GCSE OCR Double Award
Applied Science
The Workbook

This book is for anyone doing **GCSE OCR Applied Science (Double Award)** at foundation level.

GCSE Science is all about **understanding how science works**. And not only that — understanding it well enough to be able to **question** what you hear on TV and read in the papers.

But you can't do that without a fair chunk of **background knowledge**. Hmm, tricky.

This book is full of **tricky questions**... each one designed to make you sweat — because that's the only way you'll get any **better**.

There are questions to see **what facts** you know. There are questions to see how well you can **apply those facts**. And there are questions to see how well you understand the role of **scientists** in the **real world**.

It's also got some daft bits in to try and make the whole experience at least vaguely entertaining for you.

What CGP is all about

Our sole aim here at CGP is to produce the highest quality books — carefully written, immaculately presented and dangerously close to being funny.

Then we work our socks off to get them out to you — at the cheapest possible prices.

Contents

Section 2.1 — Living Organisms

Products from Living Things 1
Cells and Classification 3
Genes and Chromosomes 4
Variation 5
What Plants Need 6
Intensive Farming 10
Organic Farming 11
Comparing Farming Methods 12
Food Chains and Webs 15
Environmental Change 16
Selective Breeding 18
Genetic Engineering 19

Section 2.2 — Humans as Living Organisms

Respiration 20
Energy for Exercise 21
The Respiratory System: Breathing 22
The Respiratory System: Gas Exchange 23
The Circulatory System: Blood 24
The Circulatory System: The Heart 25
The Nervous System 26
Maintaining Constant Temperature 27
Hormones and Blood Sugar 28
Infectious Diseases 30
The Spread of Infectious Disease 31
Preventing the Spread of Infectious Disease 33
The Body Fighting Off Disease 35
Immunisation 36
Use of Drugs to Treat Disease 39
Recreational Drugs 42
Genetic Disorders 45
Mixed Questions for Sections 2.1 and 2.2 46

Section 2.3 — Obtaining Useful Chemicals

Classifying Chemicals 49
Chemical Symbols and Notation 50
Chemical Building Blocks 51
Compounds and Formulas 52
Organic and Inorganic Chemicals 53
Useful Chemicals From Rocks 54
Extracting Metals From Rocks 57
Industrial Production of Chemicals 59

Section 2.4 — Chemical and Material Behaviour

Useful Mixtures 62
Chemical Bonding and Properties 64
Ceramics 66
Polymers 68
Metals 70
Metal Recycling and Composites 72
Developing New Materials 74
Matching Properties and Uses 75
Mixed Questions for Sections 2.3 and 2.4 77

Section 2.5 — Energy, Electricity and Radiation

Fossil Fuels 79
Alternative Energy Resources 81
Energy Transfer 84
Generating Electricity 85
Energy in the Home 86
Using Energy Efficiently 87
Sankey Diagrams 90
Calculating Power and Current 91
Calculating Energy Usage and Cost 92
Heat Transfer 94
Heat Transfer in the Home 96
Heat Exchangers 98
Electromagnetic Waves 99
Uses of Electromagnetic Waves 100

Section 2.6 — The Earth and the Universe

The Earth's Atmosphere 102
Monitoring Atmospheric Change 103
Tectonic Plates 105
The Universe and its Origins 106
Mixed Questions for Sections 2.5 and 2.6 107

Published by Coordination Group Publications Ltd.

Editors:
Ellen Bowness, Tom Cain, Katherine Craig, Rose Parkin, Katherine Reed, Rachel Selway, Laurence Stamford, Jane Towle.

Contributors:
Bridie Begbie, Mike Bossart, Steve Coggins, Jane Davies, Mark A Edwards, Sarah Evans, James Foster, Dr. Iona M J Hamilton, Derek Harvey, Rebecca Harvey, Judith Hayes, Frederick Langridge, Barbara Mascetti, Andy Rankin, Philip Rushworth, Adrian Schmit, Sidney Stringer Community School, Claire Stebbing, Sophie Watkins, Jim Wilson, Chris Workman, Dee Wyatt.

ISBN: 978 1 84146 614 9

With thanks to Kate Houghton, Ami Snelling and Sarah Williams for the proofreading.
With thanks to Laura Phillips for the copyright research.

Data on page 43 reproduced with kind permission from the British Heart Foundation © 2007.

Data for Graph on page 104 reproduced with kind permission from Earth System Research Laboratory, National Oceanic and Atmospheric Administration, and Scripps Institution of Oceanography, University of California.

Groovy website: www.cgpbooks.co.uk

Printed by Elanders Hindson Ltd, Newcastle upon Tyne.
Jolly bits of clipart from CorelDRAW®

Text, design, layout and original illustrations © Coordination Group Publications Ltd. 2007
All rights reserved.

Section 2.1 — Living Organisms

Products from Living Things

Q1 Sharon likes to make her own **wine**. The diagram on the right shows the equipment that she uses.

a) Complete the **word equation** for fermentation in yeast.

glucose ⟶ .... + ...

b) Whilst the wine is fermenting Sharon needs to keep it **warm**. Why is this?

....

c) The water trap stops **air** entering the jar. Why is this important?

Think about the conditions needed for fermentation.

....

Q2 **Barton Bakery** are baking their famous bacon-flavoured loaves of **bread**. One of the most important ingredients when making bread is **yeast**.

a) What would happen to Barton Bakery's bread if they **didn't** add any yeast?

....

b) What **gas**, produced by the fermentation in yeast, causes small holes to form in the bread?

....

Q3 Reg is the head brewer at a **brewery**. He supervises the manufacture of **beer** from **grain** (such as barley).

a) Circle the correct word(s) from each pair to complete the paragraph below on **fermentation**.

> Yeast contains enzymes / alcohol. Enzymes are biological catalysts / microorganisms which slow down / speed up reactions. Without enzymes, fermentation, which is used in beer / shampoo production, would be too fast / slow to be useful. To work, fermentation needs the right temperature / lighting conditions, enough sugar and lots of / no oxygen.

b) What **substance** in the barley is converted into alcohol by the yeast?

....

Products from Living Things

Q4 Daisy has a **strawberry yoghurt** in her packed lunch.
The label on the pot says her yoghurt is made from milk.

Complete the paragraph below using the words provided to describe how Daisy's yoghurt has been manufactured. Each word can be used more than once.

sugar   heated   clot   acid   bacteria

A culture of .... is added to some milk and the mixture is .... to the right temperature. The enzymes in the .... convert the .... in the milk into ...., which causes the milk to .... and solidify into yoghurt.

Q5 A **cheese manufacturer** is making a batch of Froggarts' mature cheddar.

a) Number the boxes so that the sentences are in the correct order to explain the cheese making process.

☐ More bacteria are added and the curds are left to ripen.

☐ A culture of bacteria is added to warm milk.

☐ The bacteria cause the formation of curds in the milk.

b) The enzymes in the bacteria convert the **sugar** in the milk into what substance? ....

Q6 Complete the table to show whether each of the following products comes from **plants**, **animals** or **microorganisms** and give a **possible use** of each.

	Comes from	Used for
Leather		
Wool		
Silk		
Chemicals to make drugs, e.g. aspirin		
Cotton		
Pigments for dyes		
Medicines, e.g. penicillin		

Section 2.1 — Living Organisms

Cells and Classification

Q1 Dr Pacini is a **botanist**. He studies **plant cells** to see how they function.

a) Circle the correct word(s) to complete the sentences below.

  i) All living things are made from cells / vacuoles, the basic unit of life / proteins.

  ii) Each cell is made up of glucose / chemical compounds.

b) i) Write in the names of the parts of the plant cell labelled in the diagram below.

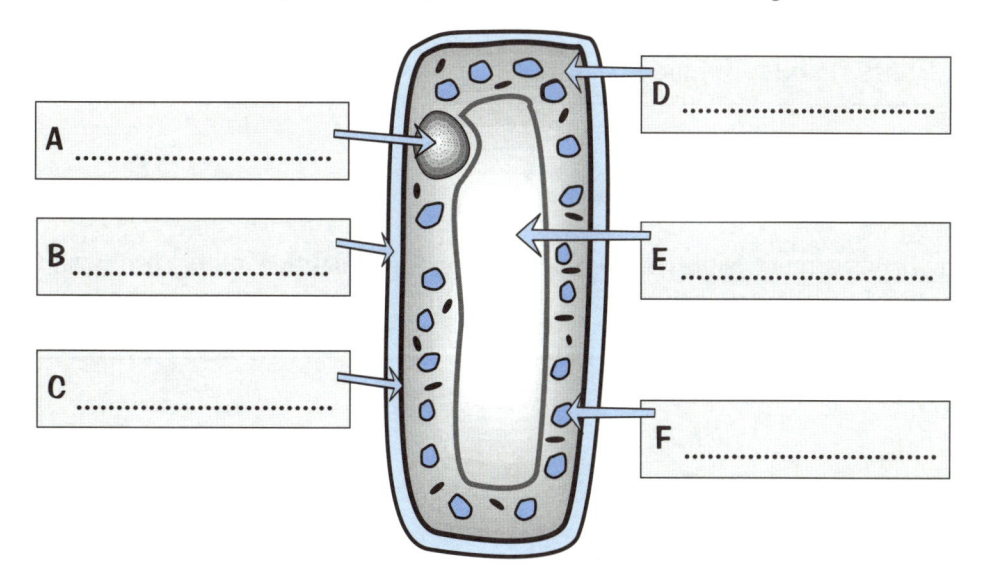

A ....
B ....
C ....
D ....
E ....
F ....

  ii) Write the letters A to F in the boxes to link the parts of the cell shown above with their function.

  ☐ The place where many chemical processes happen.
  ☐ Contains cell sap and helps provide support.
  ☐ Contains the genetic information.
  ☐ Absorbs light energy for photosynthesis.
  ☐ Controls the movement of substances in and out of the cell.
  ☐ Provides support.

  iii) Which **three** parts (A, B, C, D, E or F) are not found in **animal** cells? ....

Q2 Sheila is a **taxonomist**, a type of scientist that **classifies** organisms.

Fill in the blanks using the words given to complete the passage on the classification of organisms.

| physical | differences | identify |

Organisms are classified into groups by looking at the .... similarities and .... between them. These can then be used by scientists to .... organisms.

Section 2.1 — Living Organisms

Genes and Chromosomes

Q1 Geneticists study the genetic material inside cells, as well as the way in which different characteristics are inherited. By looking at cells, geneticists can sometimes identify abnormalities in the genetic material.

Complete the passage below by circling the correct word in each pair.

> Most cells contain strands of genetic information on long / short,
> thread-like structures called proteins / chromosomes.
> These strands are made of strings of genes / nuclei.

Q2 During IVF treatment, embryos are checked for abnormalities in the chromosomes. A geneticist extracts one cell to study. The embryo is shown below.

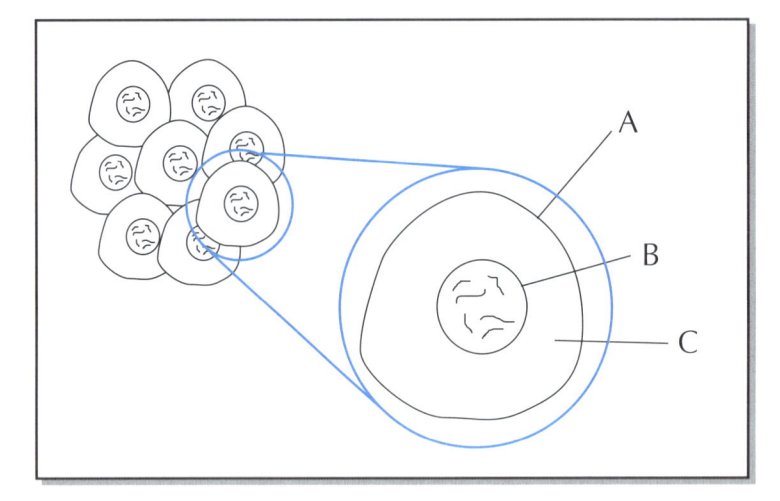

a) Which part of the cell contains the **chromosomes**? Circle the correct answer.

A   B   C

b) What is the **name** for this part of a cell? ....

c) Each chromosome contains many **genes**. What do genes do?

....

d) Write down the following in order of size, giving the smallest first and the largest last:

gene   cell   chromosome   nucleus

....

Top Tips: People often mention **DNA** when talking about genes and chromosomes, but don't worry, DNA isn't anything too fancy — it's just the **chemical** that genes are made from. There are about 25,000 genes in **you** — that's an awful lot of DNA to carry around with you. Tiring eh...

Section 2.1 — Living Organisms

Variation

Q1 Keisha's mum has black **hair** and her dad has blonde hair. Keisha's hair is also blonde.

a) Tick the boxes to show whether the following statements are true or false.

	True	False
Characteristics like hair colour are passed on from our parents in their genes.	☐	☐
The genes in your nuclei are a mixture of your parents' genes.	☐	☐
The genes in your nuclei are an exact copy of your mum's genes.	☐	☐
Gametes are produced by meiosis.	☐	☐
Characteristics are passed from one generation to the next through sexual reproduction.	☐	☐
Gametes contain twice as many chromosomes as a fertilised egg.	☐	☐

b) Keisha's sister's hair is brown. Fill in the blanks using the words provided to complete the paragraph on variation.

shuffled   gametes   fertilisation   meiosis   variation

Sexual reproduction leads to variation in the offspring by two processes:

1. During .... reproductive cells split in two to make .... and the genes get .... up.

2. During .... any two gametes, both with shuffled genes, can come together, creating even more ....

Q2 Professor Baumberg is a **geneticist** studying **reproduction** in yeast. Yeast reproduce asexually, which means they reproduce themselves by **dividing** to form **two identical** cells.

a) What is the **name** of the process by which cells copy themselves by dividing in two? Circle the correct answer.

Gamete production   Meiosis   Sexual reproduction   Mitosis   Fertilisation

b) What is this process used for in humans? Circle the **two** correct answers.

Growth   Variation   Fertilisation   Repairing damaged cells/tissues

Section 2.1 — Living Organisms

What Plants Need

Q1 Dominic is an **agricultural consultant** who advises farmers on how to increase crop yield. He says that sunlight is very important because plants produce their own '**food**' using **sunlight**.

a) What is the **name** of the process that plants use to produce their own 'food'?

....

b) Fill in the blanks to complete the word equation for the process plants use to produce their own 'food'.

.... + ... $\xrightarrow[\text{chlorophyll}]{\text{light}}$ .... + ...

c) Complete the passage below using the words provided.

| carbon dioxide | light | leaves | water | chlorophyll |

Photosynthesis occurs mainly in the .... It requires four main things:

1. .... enters leaves from the surrounding air.

2. .... is drawn up from the soil.

3. .... from the Sun provides energy.

4. Energy is absorbed by a green substance found in chloroplasts, called ....

Q2 New potato plants are grown from potato **tubers**, which are high in **starch**.

a) i) Draw lines to link the substance with the correct statement.

Starch — This substance is a soluble sugar that can be transported around plants.

Glucose — This substance is an insoluble sugar that is stored in plants.

ii) Circle the correct word from each pair to complete the sentence below.

If starch / glucose is not needed immediately it can be converted into glucose / starch.

b) i) The tubers require **energy** to grow. What is the name of the **process** which releases energy?

....

ii) Tick the boxes to show whether each statement about this process is true or false.

	True	False
Carbon dioxide and water are waste products.	☐	☐
Glucose is first broken down to starch.	☐	☐
It requires oxygen from the air.	☐	☐
Oxygen is a waste product of this process.	☐	☐

Section 2.1 — Living Organisms

What Plants Need

Q3 Richard grows house plants **commercially** for sale to garden centres. Over the years Richard has spent a lot of money building **glass houses** in which to grow his plants.

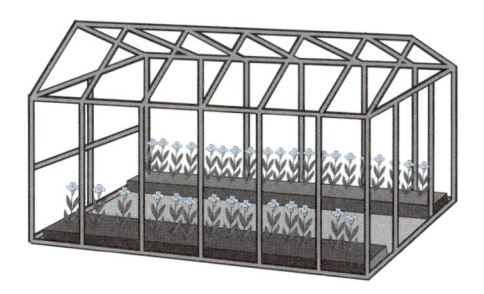

a) Richard **burns fuel** in his glass houses to increase the air temperature, making his plants grow faster.

   i) Why does **increasing** the air temperature make the plants grow faster?

   ....

   ....

   ii) In **addition** to heat, what does burning fuel produce?

   ....

   iii) Why does this other product help Richard's plants to grow **faster**?

   ....

   ....

b) Richard's glass houses also have **artificial lighting**.

   i) **When** would Richard use the artificial lighting?

   ....

   ii) What **benefit** does the artificial lighting provide?

   ....

   ....

c) Last year, Richard also grew some house plants outside. He noticed that his plants grew **faster** in the **summer**. Give **two** reasons why plants grow faster in the summer than they do in winter.

   1. .... 2. ....

d) Even though Richard planted the same number of house plants inside and outside, not as many grew outside. He noticed that lots of **weeds** had grown around his outside plants. Suggest why the weeds may have led to fewer plants growing outside.

   ....

Section 2.1 — Living Organisms

What Plants Need

Q4 The following passage is taken from an information leaflet produced by a **fertiliser manufacturer** explaining why **minerals** are important to plants.

Circle the correct word from each pair to complete the passage.

> Plants get the minerals / acid they need for healthy growth from the air / soil. Minerals in the soil are in solution (i.e. dissolved in oxygen / water), which is absorbed by the plant's flowers / roots. If a plant doesn't get enough minerals it can suffer from deficiency / hunger symptoms. Gardeners can add fertilisers / water to the soil to make sure that their plants get all the minerals they need. Different fertilisers contain different amounts of soil / minerals so that gardeners can choose the one that's best for their plants.

Q5 Vicky is a **garden consultant** — she visits people's gardens to advise them on how to **improve** the **growth** of their plants and lawns.

Many of the problems Vicky sees can be solved using **fertilisers** rich in particular minerals. For each of the problems in the table below, write down which type of **mineral** the fertiliser should contain a high concentration of. The first one has been done for you.

Problem	Vicky thinks this is caused by	Fertiliser should contain mostly
Pauline's plum trees were producing only very small plums.	A problem with the plant's enzymes.	potassium
The leaves on John's pansies turned purple as they got older.	Poor root growth — the plants were not able to respire properly.	
The leaves on Arthur's sweet peas started to discolour.	A problem with the plant's enzymes.	
Brenda planted some lilies, but the leaves came out yellow.	Plants were lacking the green pigment chlorophyll.	
All the plants in Edith's garden have stunted growth. As they got older their leaves turned yellow.	The plant cannot produce enough of the right proteins.	

Top Tips: Gardeners (and farmers) use fertilisers to prevent deficiency (e.g. stunted growth). You need to be able to interpret which mineral is lacking from the different problems a plant shows.

Section 2.1 — Living Organisms

What Plants Need

Q6 Zulfi is training to become an **agricultural scientist**. He has to learn all about the different **minerals** that plants need for **healthy growth**.

Draw lines to link the following minerals with the reason why plants require them.

Nitrates	Needed for making chlorophyll, which is needed for photosynthesis.
Phosphates	Needed to make proteins, which are needed for cell growth.
Potassium	Needed for healthy growth and flowering.
Magnesium	Needed for healthy growth, especially of roots.

Q7 A scientist was investigating the symptoms of **mineral deficiency** in plants. She planted six **identical** seeds in test tubes containing various types of **fertiliser**, as shown below. The seeds were grown for two weeks.

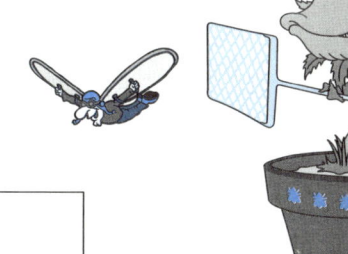

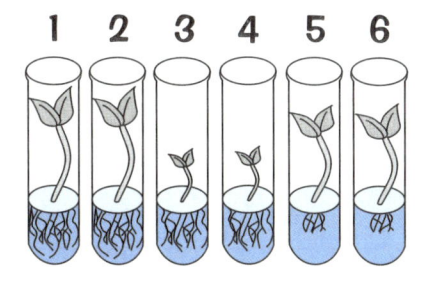

Tubes' Key
1 and 2: complete mineral content
3 and 4: low in mineral A
5 and 6: low in mineral B

a) Suggest why tubes 1 and 2 were included.

....

b) Draw lines to link the number of the tubes to the main deficiency symptom they were showing.

Tubes 3 and 4   Poor root growth

Tubes 5 and 6   Stunted growth

c) Predict which mineral the plants in the following tubes were lacking:

i) 3 and 4 ....

ii) 5 and 6 ....

d) Suggest why all the minerals required **except one** were supplied to tubes 3, 4, 5 and 6.

....
....

Section 2.1 — Living Organisms

Intensive Farming

Q1 Simon recently inherited the family farm. An **agricultural consultant** has advised him to introduce **intensive farming methods** on the farm in order to increase his **crop yield**.

a) Complete the paragraph below to explain exactly what is meant by the term 'intensive farming'.

> high   maximum   yields   minimum   low

Intensive farming methods are used by farmers to produce bigger and better .... The aim is to get the .... amount of food from the .... possible amount of land. One advantage of intensive farming is that a wide variety of .... quality foods can be produced at .... prices.

b) Simon plans to use **artificial fertilisers** on his land to increase the crop yield. Explain how artificial fertilisers help increase crop yield.

....
....
....

Simon's farming methods were intense

c) Simon intends to use **artificial pesticides**, **fungicides** and **herbicides** on the farm. Complete the table below to explain what each one does and how it will increase the amount of crops Simon produces.

Chemical	What it does	How it improves yield
		Prevents mould damage to crops
	Kills weeds	
Pesticide		

Q2 Jack is a poultry farmer. He intensively farms **chickens**. Explain how intensive farming can **increase meat production**.

....
....
....

Section 2.1 — Living Organisms

Organic Farming

Q1 Farms that are organic can be certified by the **Soil Association**.
Organic farmers use more **traditional methods** of farming than intensive farmers.

   a) Describe how **animals** are kept on organic farms compared to intensive farms.

   ....

   b) In order to keep soil fertile, organic farmers use **natural fertilisers** instead of artificial fertilisers.

     i) What are **natural** fertilisers?

     ....

     ii) Give **one** advantage of using natural fertilisers instead of artificial fertilisers.

     ....

     iii) Give **one** disadvantage of using natural fertilisers instead of artificial fertilisers.

     ....

Q2 Hugh has been farming **organically** for the past eight years.
Everything grown on his farm carries the Soil Association logo.

   a) Circle the correct word from each pair in the paragraph below
to explain how Hugh controls **pests** on his farm.

> For high crop yields, it is important to kill pests / weeds that eat crops. If a farm is classed as organic, artificial herbicides / pesticides cannot be used to kill pests. Instead, natural / artificial pesticides are used, which don't affect the pests / environment as much, as long as they are used responsibly. Pests can also be killed by using artificial / biological control. A predator / prey is introduced that kills the pest, instead of using fertilisers / chemicals.

   b) Hugh's farm is classed as organic so he cannot use artificial chemicals to control weeds.

     i) What method would an organic farmer use to **control weeds**?

     ....

     ii) Give one **disadvantage** of the method of organic weed control you stated above.

     ....

     ....

Section 2.1 — Living Organisms

Comparing Farming Methods

Q1 Nigel works for the **Environment Agency**. He's investigating reports that a **stream** (which runs alongside a farmer's land) has become covered in a thick blanket of **algae**.

a) i) What **substance** used in agriculture could be the cause of this algal growth?

....

ii) When Nigel analyses the water he finds that the concentrations of **one** mineral are significantly higher than the others. Which **mineral** is this most likely to be? Circle the correct answer.

    Magnesium   Nitrate   Potassium

b) i) Put the following sentences in order to describe the problems that this algal growth will cause. The first one has been done for you.

- [ ] Fish die.
- [1] Blanket of algae blocks out sunlight.
- [ ] Decomposers feed on dead plants.
- [ ] Plants die.
- [ ] All the oxygen in the water is used up.

ii) What is the **name** of this process? ....

Q2 Amanda works for an environmental consultancy firm. She recently collected samples of **dead organisms** from a pond. She analyses them for the presence of **pesticides**. The diagram below shows the **concentrations** of pesticide Amanda found in each organism.

Concentration of pesticide in microscopic algae: 0.05 ppm → Concentration of pesticide in microscopic animals: 4 ppm → Concentration of pesticide in small fish: 500 ppm → Concentration of pesticide in eels: 2500 ppm

a) Suggest **where** the pesticide that contaminated the pond might have come from.

....

b) How many times more **concentrated** was the pesticide in eels than in the microscopic algae?

....

c) Only a low concentration of pesticide was present in the water.
Explain why the concentration of pesticide in eels is so **high**.

....

....

Section 2.1 — Living Organisms

Comparing Farming Methods

Q3 Read the following passage about organic farming and answer the questions that follow.

> Why does organic food cost so much? Well, it costs more for the farmer to grow crops, partly because it's more labour-intensive. Organic farmers don't use herbicides — so they have to pay people to weed their crops by hand. The use of pesticides is also restricted in organic farming — so the organic farmer risks losing his crops when they get munched up by pests like slugs.
>
> The yield from organic agriculture is lower than from conventional farming. In other words, you get fewer carrots per acre of field. Organic methods rely on growing healthy plants and animals at an unforced pace. For instance, intensively farmed pigs are fed antibiotics, which prevent the spread of disease but which also make them grow faster. Organically farmed pigs are just fed pig food — so they take longer to grow big and become ready for slaughter. Also, organically produced animals are given space to roam around. Intensively farmed animals are often confined in small cages — this uses much less land, so it's cheaper.
>
> So why pay all that extra money — is intensive farming so dreadful? Well, if you like to hear birds singing and see wild flowers and butterflies, blasting the countryside with weedkiller and pesticides is probably not wise. And 'factory farming' isn't much fun if you're a pig or a chicken. It's cheap of course, but it could bring trouble in the long run.

a) What **two** products are organic farmers **not** allowed to use?

   1. ....   2. ....

b) Give **two** reasons why intensive farming produces more food than organic farming.

   1. ....

   2. ....

c) Why might some people prefer to buy meat that has been farmed organically rather than meat that has been farmed intensively?

   ....

   ....

d) Many governments are currently trying to encourage farmers to adopt organic farming practices.

   i) Give **one** reason why a government might want to increase the number of organic farms.

   ....

   ii) State **two** reasons why many farmers don't change from intensive to organic farming.

   1. ....

   2. ....

Section 2.1 — Living Organisms

Comparing Farming Methods

Q4 Robert has been **intensively farming** carrots for many years. He's worried that the consequences of using fertilisers may be **hazardous to health**.

a) Tick the boxes to show whether the following statements are true or false.

	True	False
Excessive nitrates in drinking water are good for your health.	☐	☐
Excessive nitrates in drinking water can cause serious health problems.	☐	☐
Nitrates enter reservoirs from excess fertilisers.	☐	☐
Nitrates prevent the blood from carrying oxygen properly.	☐	☐

b) Give **two** disadvantages, other than affecting health, of intensive farming.

1. ....

2. ....

Q5 Some farmers are changing from **intensive farming** methods to more **traditional methods**.

a) Draw lines to match the pairs of statements below to show the **advantages** of organic farming.

- Artificial pesticides aren't used — animals are treated more ethically.
- No battery farming — there is less risk of chemicals remaining on food.
- Chemical herbicides and fungicides aren't used — there is less disruption to food chains.

b) Complete the paragraph below about organic farming by circling the correct word in each pair.

> Organic farming requires **less / more** space than intensive farming. It is **more / less** labour-intensive, which **increases / decreases** production costs. Overall, organic farming produces **less / more** food than intensive farming for the same area of land.

Top Tips: In the exam they might ask you to compare different farming methods — that means you need to know the **pros** and **cons** of organic and intensive farming inside out. Fun... Also, make sure you give a balanced argument in the exam, whatever your opinion might be.

Section 2.1 — Living Organisms

Food Chains and Webs

Q1 Boris has recently become a farmer, and has chosen to grow **wheat**. Unfortunately, he has found that **cockroaches** are eating some of his crop. The **food chain** is shown below.

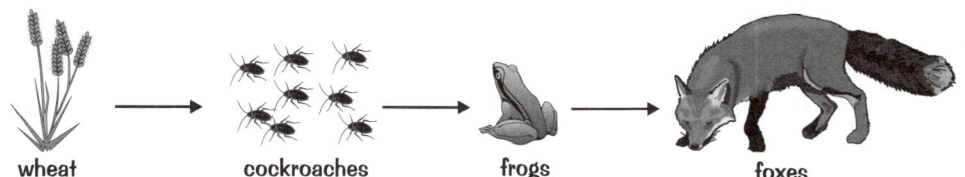

wheat → cockroaches → frogs → foxes

a) Boris decides to spray the cockroaches with a **pesticide** to control the size of their population. Explain what effect this could have on:

   i) the wheat population. ....
   ....

   ii) the frog population. ....
   ....

b) Draw lines to match three of the organisms in this food chain to their role in the food chain.

   frogs   producer
   wheat   secondary consumer
   cockroaches primary consumer

c) Suggest why there are only four trophic levels in this food chain.

   ....
   ....

Q2 The diagram on the right shows a **woodland food web**. Last year a chemical was spilt in the woods, which turned out to be poisonous to voles. The population of **voles** significantly **decreased**.

a) Suggest an explanation for each of the following consequences:

   i) The population of barn owls **decreasing**.
   ....

   ii) The population of insects **increasing**.
   ....

b) Suggest what might happen to the **bird population**. Give a reason for your answer.

....
....

Section 2.1 — Living Organisms

Environmental Change

Q1 The diagram shows part of a food web from Nebraska in the USA. The **flowerhead weevil** doesn't occur naturally in this area. It was introduced by **farmers** to eat the musk thistle, which is a weed.

a) What effect will the introduction of the flowerhead weevil have on the amount of wild honey produced by honeybees in the area? Give a reason for your answer.

....

....

b) Suggest a reason why the population of platte thistles may increase as the population of musk thistles is reduced by the introduction of flowerhead weevils.

....

....

Q2 Sally is studying what factors affect the **flowering time** of a certain species of plant. She discovers that the plant starts to flower when the temperature reaches **20 °C**. The table shows Sally's results.

year	1980	1985	1990	1995	2000
month when plant starts to flower	July	July	June	June	May

a) Describe the trend seen in the results.

....

b) i) What does this suggest about the time of year when the temperature reaches 20 °C?

....

ii) Suggest a reason for this.

....

c) Explain the effect this trend may have on the animals that feed on these flowers.

....

....

Section 2.1 — Living Organisms

Environmental Change

Q3 Jimmy is studying the **hibernation** behaviour of **hedgehogs** in his area — he thinks that it's being affected by **climate change**. He knows that hedgehogs begin to hibernate once air temperatures drop below a certain level. This year, he finds that many hedgehogs haven't hibernated.

a) Suggest a reason why many hedgehogs haven't hibernated.

....

b) How might this affect the population of hedgehogs? Circle the correct word(s) in each pair.

Their population size might increase / decrease because
there's not as much / more food available in winter.

c) What effects might this have on the food chain that the hedgehogs are part of in the local area?

....

....

Q4 Roneeta is an **oceanographer**. She's concerned that the burning of **fossil fuels** is causing the sea to **warm** and that this is affecting the **distribution** of dolphins. The **common dolphin** is adapted to live in **warm waters** near the equator. The **white-beaked dolphin** is adapted to inhabit **colder**, more northerly waters.

a) Suggest how a rise in sea temperature could affect the common dolphin.

....

b) Suggest how a rise in sea temperature could affect the white-beaked dolphin.

....

Q5 Organisms need to be able to survive in a **changing environment** caused by **climate change**. Complete the passage using words from the box. Some words may be used more than once.

| offspring | variation | differences | trait | common | survive |

Organisms within a species all have slight .... These are known as .... If a population's environment changes, some individuals will be able to cope because they have a .... that allows them to .... Those that .... will pass on the .... to their offspring. They will then be able to .... in the new environment and the .... will become .... in the population.

Section 2.1 — Living Organisms

Selective Breeding

Q1 Jeremy is a **beef farmer**. To maximise his profits he **selectively breeds** cows that have the highest meat yields.

a) Number the sentences below to show the stages of selective breeding in the correct order.

- [ ] Breed them with each other (cross-breeding).
- [ ] Select the best offspring.
- [ ] Continue the process over many generations.
- [ ] Combine with the best you already have and breed again.
- [1] Select individuals with the best characteristics.

b) Complete the following sentences by circling the correct word(s) in each pair.

i) Selective breeding **increases** / decreases the number of variations of a gene in a population.

ii) Animals in a herd that have been bred selectively will be **closely** / distantly related.

iii) If a new disease appears few / **all** of the animals are likely to be affected.

iv) There's **more** / less chance of organisms developing genetic diseases.

Q2 Sarah has just inherited a **dairy farm**. A local farmer has offered her a choice of bulls to **breed** with her cows.

a) Circle **two** characteristics that Sarah should look for in the bulls.

Good disease resistance   High milk yield in the bull's mother   Bad-tempered   Low fertility

The graph shows the milk yield for Sarah's cows over the last three generations.

b) From the graph, do you think that **selective breeding** is likely to have been used with these cows? Explain your answer.

....

....

....

c) What is the **increase** in the average milk yield per cow from generation 1 to generation 3?

....

d) Sarah is also considering growing **fruit** on her farm. Suggest one characteristic that she is likely to look for when choosing plants to breed together.

....

Section 2.1 — Living Organisms

Genetic Engineering

Q1 Agricultural scientists can use genetic engineering to modify plants and animals to have desirable characteristics. Complete the passage below using words in the box to describe the process of genetic engineering.

| characteristics | cells | foreign | plants | gene |

Genetic engineering is where .... genes are transferred into the .... of animals, ... or microorganisms. The new .... that organisms displays depends on the type of .... inserted.

Q2 Heather is a member of a group that campaigns **against** genetically engineered foods.

a) Suggest **two** reasons why Heather might think that genetic engineering is **ethically** wrong.

1. ....

2. ....

b) Tick **two** advantages of genetic engineering.

- [ ] The gene used could escape.
- [ ] Crops could be produced with added vitamins.
- [ ] Crops could be produced to be more susceptible to disease.
- [ ] Animals could be produced that would grow more quickly.

Q3 Below are some statements that different people have made about **genetically modified (GM) plants**. In each case, say whether they are making an argument **for** or **against** GM technology.

a) "Genes newly inserted into crop plants, for example for pest-resistance, may spread to nearby wild plants." — Gregory Greene, conservationist. ....

b) "**Some people could develop allergic reactions to foods that have been genetically modified**." — Jermaine Eaton, nutritionist. ....

c) "We can produce rice plants containing toxins that are harmful to locusts but not to people." — Veronica Speedwell, biotechnology consultant. ....

d) "**By using herbicide-resistant crops on my land, I can kill all the weeds in my field with a single dose of all-purpose herbicide**." — Ed Jones, farmer. ....

e) "Investing in improving traditional agricultural methods will improve yields more than investment in GM technology." — Abigail Singh, relief worker. ....

Section 2.1 — Living Organisms

Section 2.2 — Humans as Living Organisms

Respiration

Q1 Doctor Khan is a **sports scientist**. He's investigating how the activity of athletes affects their rate of respiration.

a) Explain what is meant by the term **respiration**.

....

b) Complete the following word equation for aerobic respiration:

glucose + ... → **carbon dioxide** + ... (+ **energy**)

c) Give **three** things that the energy released by respiration is used for.

....

....

d) Complete the flow charts by filling in the blanks using the words below. You may need to use some words more than once.

blood   cells   circulatory   glucose   digestive   oxygen

i)
The sugary food you eat is digested into .... and moves from the .... system into the ....

⬇

The .... then carries the .... to the ....

ii)
Breathing in moves .... into your lungs.

⬇

The .... then moves into the ....

⬇

.... moves around the body in the .... system to the ....

Energy For Exercise

Q1 Humans can respire **aerobically** — but if there isn't enough oxygen available we can also respire **anaerobically**.

a) Give **one** advantage of aerobic respiration over anaerobic respiration.

....

....

b) In what circumstances would a human start respiring anaerobically?

....

....

c) Write the **word equation** for anaerobic respiration in humans.

.... → .... + ...

Q2 Jim is a keen runner. He takes part in a 400 metre race. The **graph** below shows Jim's **breathing rate** before, during and after the race.

a) What was Jim's **peak** breathing rate? ....

Think about what's breathed in and what it's used for.

b) Why does Jim's breathing rate increase during the race?

....

....

c) Jim noticed that his **pulse rate** increased during the race. Why does pulse rate increase during exercise?

....

....

Section 2.2 — Humans as Living Organisms

The Respiratory System: Breathing

Q1 Many people suffer from problems with the **respiratory system**, so it's important for **doctors** to learn about the structure of the thorax.

Draw lines to match the letters from the diagram with their correct names.

A — diaphragm muscle
B — lung
C — intercostal muscle
D — bronchus
E — trachea
F — bronchiole
G — rib
H — alveoli

Q2 Dr Baker uses a **peak flow meter** to assess whether a patient is asthmatic. The patient is asked to breathe out hard into the equipment.

a) Fill in the blanks in the passage below to show what happens when the patient **breathes out**.

| increases | thorax | decreases | intercostal | diaphragm | relax |

When the patient breathes out, a muscle below the chest called the .... relaxes and moves up. This .... the volume of the thorax, forcing air out of the lungs. The .... muscles (the muscles between the ribs) also .... when breathing out.

b) Number the following structures (1-6) in order to show the route that oxygen takes when the patient breathes out into the peak flow meter. The first one has been done for you.

☐ bronchiole   [1] alveolus
☐ bronchus   ☐ peak flow meter
☐ trachea   ☐ mouth cavity

Top Tips: It's not the easiest thing to get your head around — all that contracting and relaxing, and the changes in thorax volume. If you make sure you know all the parts of the respiratory system and how they cause air to move in and out, you'll be breathing easy in the exam.

Section 2.2 — Humans as Living Organisms

The Respiratory System: Gas Exchange

Q1 **Emphysema** is a lung disease where the walls of the **alveoli** are damaged. This affects **gas exchange**.

a) The diagram shows an alveolus and capillary. Match the labels A-D with the following statements:

i) air in ☐

ii) air out ☐

iii) movement of CO_2 ☐

iv) movement of O_2 ☐

b) By what **process** does the exchange of oxygen and carbon dioxide occur?

....

Q2 Complete the passage using words from the box below.

| respiratory system | oxygen | blood | carbon dioxide | toxic | respiration |

The process of .... produces ....

High levels of this substance in the .... is

.... and so it must be removed from the body. This is done

by the ....

Q3 The composition of **inhaled** and **exhaled air** is different.

a) Complete the following sentences by circling the correct word in each pair.

i) Exhaled air contains **more** / **less** oxygen than inhaled air.

ii) Exhaled air contains **more** / **less** carbon dioxide than inhaled air.

iii) Exhaled air contains **more** / **less** moisture than inhaled air.

iv) Exhaled air is usually **warmer** / **colder** than inhaled air.

b) Complete the table to show the approximate percentages of nitrogen, oxygen and carbon dioxide in inhaled and exhaled air.

17%   79%   4%   79%   21%   0.04%

	Inhaled air	Exhaled air
Nitrogen		
Oxygen		
Carbon dioxide		

Section 2.2 — Humans as Living Organisms

The Circulatory System: Blood

Q1 When Jamie had a **blood test**, his **doctor** explained to him the importance of blood in the body.

Tick the box next to any statements that describe a function of the blood.

☐ Transporting carbon dioxide to the cells.

☐ Removing waste products from the cells.

☐ Taking waste products to the cells.

☐ Transporting oxygen and food to the cells.

Q2 A **nurse** took a sample of **blood** from a patient and sent it to the hospital laboratory for **analysis**. The results of his analysis are shown below.

> Number of red blood cells per mm^3 = 6 million
>
> Number of white blood cells per mm^3 = 6000
>
> Number of platelets per mm^3 = 100 000

...five million, nine hundred and ninety eight thousand, nine hundred and seventy... Oh drat I've lost count... One, two, three...

a) How many times more red blood cells are there, than white blood cells?

....

b) Draw lines to match each component of blood with its main function.

red blood cells	help the blood to clot at the site of a wound
white blood cells	protect the body from harmful microorganisms
platelets	transport oxygen from the lungs to the rest of the body

c) i) What is the name of the liquid that carries platelets, red blood cells and white blood cells around in the blood?

....

ii) Name two other substances that are transported by this liquid.

1. ....

2. ....

Top Tips: Blood isn't just there in case a hungry vampire comes along — it has some pretty important jobs in the body. It's a good idea to make sure you know what some of these are, and also to know what blood's made up of. It's not just a red liquid — there are all sorts of things in there.

Section 2.2 — Humans as Living Organisms

The Circulatory System: The Heart

Q1 John visited a **cardiologist** after experiencing chest pains.
The cardiologist showed John a diagram of the heart.

a) The diagram below shows the human heart, as seen from the front.
The left atrium has been labelled. Complete the remaining labels A to F.

A ....
B ....
C ....
D ....
E ....
F ....

b) Describe the **function** of the parts of the heart listed below.

i) Right atrium
....

ii) Tricuspid valve
....

iii) Left ventricle
....

Q2 Danny asked his doctor about what the different parts of his **circulatory system** do.
Draw lines to match each part of the circulatory system to its purpose.

heart — where materials are exchanged between the blood and cells

arteries — pumps blood to the body and the lungs

veins — transport blood away from the heart

capillaries — transport blood to the heart

Section 2.2 — Humans as Living Organisms

The Nervous System

Q1 John has suffered **damage** to his **spinal cord**. His doctor says it has been completely severed. The diagram shows the position of the damage.

a) The spinal cord is part of the central nervous system.

i) What is the function of the central nervous system?

....

ii) What other structure makes up the central nervous system?

....

b) Suggest **how** the injury will affect John's movements.

....

....

c) Give a reason **why** the injury will affect John's movements.

....

....

....

Think about how movements are brought about in the body.

spinal cord damaged at this point

Q2 Jamie was cooking his mum some tea when he accidentally picked up a **hot** saucepan. Jamie **instantly** dropped the pan back onto the hob.

a) Put numbers in the boxes so that the following statements are in the correct order to describe how Jamie's nervous system responded to him picking up the hot pan. The first one has been done for you.

☐ Some of the muscles in Jamie's hand contract causing him to drop the pan.

[1] Temperature receptors in Jamie's hand detect the increase in temperature.

☐ Impulses travel along a motor neurone.

☐ Impulses travel along a sensory neurone.

☐ The information is processed by the spinal cord.

b) Muscles are one type of effector. Name the other type of effector.

....

Section 2.2 — Humans as Living Organisms

Maintaining Constant Temperature

Q1 Yolanda and Subarna are on holiday in **Egypt**, where the daytime **temperature** can get uncomfortably **high**.

a) Yolanda and Subarna are told that the blood vessels close to the surface of their skin get bigger in diameter in the heat.

Tick the boxes to show whether these statements are **true** or **false**.

	True	False
i) Skin looks red when it's hot due to a decrease in the blood flow to the skin.	☐	☐
ii) More heat is lost from the body to the surroundings when blood vessels close to the skin's surface are smaller in diameter.	☐	☐
iii) Vasodilation and vasoconstriction help to regulate body temperature.	☐	☐
iv) Skin looks pale in the cold because little blood is getting to its surface.	☐	☐

b) i) At what temperature do the body's reactions work best?

....

ii) What **controls** body temperature and helps to keep it constant?

....

Q2 A rescue team discovered an injured climber on a mountain ledge. The rescue team were concerned that the climber was suffering from hypothermia — a **dangerously low body temperature**.

When you are cold, your blood vessels change in order to help maintain body temperature. Circle the correct words in the passage below to describe how this works.

> When you are too cold, blood vessels close to the skin's surface get **smaller** / **larger** in diameter. This is known as **vasodilation** / **vasoconstriction**. This means that **more** / **less** blood gets to the surface of the skin. This stops the blood from **losing** / **gaining** its heat to the surroundings.

Top Tips: Your body is pretty nifty when it comes to controlling its temperature — it's not just posh cars that have climate control systems. You need to know what happens when your body gets too hot or too cold — and don't forget to use the special words, **vasodilation** and **vasoconstriction**.

Section 2.2 — Humans as Living Organisms

Hormones and Blood Sugar

Q1 Jack has recently been diagnosed with gigantism — a condition caused by having too much growth hormone. His doctor explains how **hormones function**.

Complete the passage using words from the box below.

| glands | target | blood | chemicals |

Hormones are .... that are produced in .... They are released directly into the .... They travel all over the body but only affect .... cells.

Q2 Hormones don't just cause immediate changes — they also cause **slow changes** within the body over a long period of time.

a) Give an example of a slow change in the body that is caused by hormones.

....

b) Explain why responses caused by hormones are slower than responses caused by nerve signals.

....

Q3 Helen goes to the **doctor** as she has been feeling more tired than usual. Her other symptoms include feeling very thirsty, producing excess amounts of urine and weight loss. The doctor suggests that she might have **diabetes**.

a) Diabetes is a condition caused by a deficiency of a hormone. Name this hormone.

....

b) Describe the function of this hormone.

....

c) Where is this hormone produced?

....

d) What effect does diabetes have on blood sugar levels in the body?

....

Section 2.2 — Humans as Living Organisms

Hormones and Blood Sugar

Q4 Number the stages (1-4) to show one way in which blood sugar levels decrease.

- [ ] The pancreas detects the increase in glucose level.
- [ ] Glucose is removed from the blood.
- [ ] Glucose levels rise.
- [ ] The pancreas releases insulin.

Q5 A scientist is investigating the effect of diet on blood glucose levels. The graph below shows the levels of **glucose** in the blood of two different people after they had both consumed exactly the same type of meal.

a) How many minutes after finishing the meal did the blood sugar level of person B start to decrease?

....

b) Which person, A or B, is likely to suffer from diabetes? Explain your answer.

Think about what happens to blood sugar levels in people with diabetes.

....
....

c) Give two ways that people with diabetes can control their blood glucose levels.

1. ....
2. ....

Top Tips: Hormones are pretty useful little things — they're not just what your parents use to blame your behaviour on. They're always working away to control what's going on in your body without you even having to think about it. Unfortunately, you'll need to think about this work a bit.

Section 2.2 — Humans as Living Organisms

Infectious Diseases

Q1 After eating some **leftovers** that weren't **reheated properly** Ashley has been suffering from **food poisoning**.

a) Food poisoning can be caused by pathogens. What are pathogens?
....

b) Name the two types of microorganisms below.

A. ....   B. ....

c) Tick the boxes to show whether the following statements are true or false.

	True	False
i) All bacteria cause disease.	☐	☐
ii) Bacteria don't have a nucleus.	☐	☐
iii) Bacteria are not living.	☐	☐

d) Give two ways that bacteria can make you feel ill.

1. ....   2. ....

Q2 Annie is recovering from **measles** — a disease caused by a **virus**. Number the statements below so that they are in the correct order to show how the measles virus made Annie feel **ill**.

☐ The invaded cells burst, releasing more measles viruses.

☐ The measles virus uses Annie's cells to replicate and produce more viruses.

☐ The measles virus invades Annie's cells.

☐ The new measles viruses go on to invade more of Annie's cells.

Q3 Michael is a specialist in **infectious diseases**.

Name three diseases, one caused by **bacteria**, one caused by a **virus** and one caused by **fungi**, that are not already mentioned on this page.

Bacterial infection: ....

Viral infection: ....

Fungal infection: ....

Section 2.2 — Humans as Living Organisms

The Spread of Infectious Disease

Q1 A nurse is advising people infected with **HIV** how to avoid passing on the disease. HIV can be spread by direct contact of **bodily fluids** such as **blood**.

Tick the boxes to indicate which of the following pieces of advice she should give to the patients to prevent the spread of the disease.

☐ Don't have unprotected sex.

☐ Always wash your hands before preparing food.

☐ Avoid being bitten by insects.

☐ Don't share needles.

Q2 The graph shows the change in Harry's **body temperature** during an **influenza infection**. Their temperature was recorded at the same time every day.

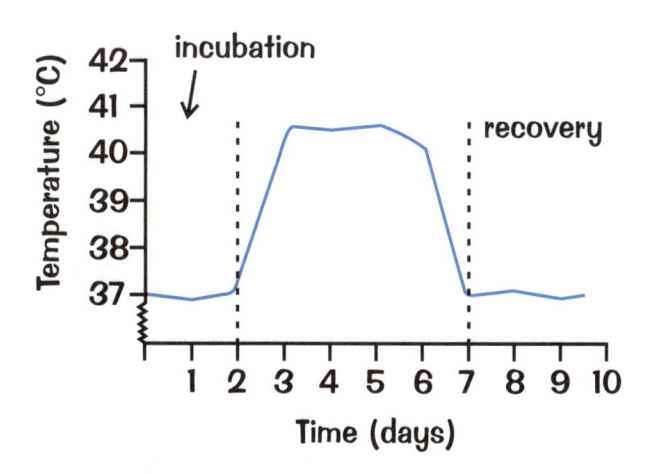

a) What was the maximum body temperature during this illness?

....

b) Approximately how many days after direct contact with someone infected with the influenza virus might you start to feel unwell?

....

c) Explain how the influenza virus is spread.

....

....

d) Suggest how the spread of this virus could be reduced.

....

Section 2.2 — Humans as Living Organisms

The Spread of Infectious Disease

Q3 Dr Spencer is setting up a **hospital** in an African country. He wants to put **prevention methods** in place in the hospital to reduce the spread of **malaria**. Malaria is a disease caused by microorganisms, which are usually spread by **mosquitos**.

a) Suggest a control measure he could put in place to try to prevent patients contracting malaria whilst staying in his hospital.

....

b) Suggest another prevention measure that Dr Spencer should advise patients to take.

....

c) How can disease be spread by insects? Circle the correct answer.

Insects create infected droplets that can pass through the air.

Insects take up microorganisms from the blood of an infected person/animal and pass them on when they bite the next person/animal.

Q4 There was an outbreak of a serious, **unknown infectious disease** in a **town**. A group of scientists investigated the spread of the disease. On the fourth day of the outbreak, they asked everyone in the town to **boil** their **drinking water** before use.

a) What was the maximum number of new cases of the disease in one day? ....

b) How soon after the town's inhabitants were advised to boil their drinking water were there no new cases reported? ....

c) How do you think the disease was spread?

....

d) Suggest why boiling drinking water had an effect on the spread of the disease.

....

Q5 A patient with an infectious disease is being kept in **isolation** in hospital in order to prevent the spread of the disease.

a) Suggest the most likely way the disease is spread. Circle the correct answer.

being bitten by an insect   droplets in the air   faecal contamination

b) How could keeping the patient in isolation prevent the spread of the disease?

....

....

Section 2.2 — Humans as Living Organisms

Preventing the Spread of Infectious Disease

Q1 Froggarts Pharmaceuticals have developed a new **antiseptic** called "Germ-no-more" that is about to be launched in shops and hospitals.

a) Fill in the gaps in the sentences below to show part of the label of "Germ-no-more".

skin	microorganisms	disinfectants	chemical

Antiseptics are .... that, unlike

...., can be used on the ....

Antiseptics kill some ....

b) Frank is a medical sales representative who is trying to sell "Germ-no-more" to a hospital. Apart from cleaning cuts, what could Frank suggest they use "Germ-no-more" for?

....

Q2 Metal **surgical equipment** is often **sterilised** using very high **temperatures**.

a) Why does surgical equipment have to be sterilised?

....

b) How do high temperatures sterilise surgical equipment?

....

c) What might be used to sterilise **plastic** surgical equipment?

Some plastics will melt if you use heat.

....

Q3 Good hygiene in **hospitals** is extremely important to **reduce** the spread of diseases such as MRSA.

a) Explain how using disinfectants helps to prevent the spread of disease in hospitals.

....

....

b) Why don't nurses use disinfectants to clean their hands?

....

c) What could nurses use instead of disinfectant to clean their hands?

....

Section 2.2 — Humans as Living Organisms

Preventing the Spread of Infectious Disease

Q4 Doctors should **wash their hands** before and after examining a patient and **wear gloves** when taking blood samples.

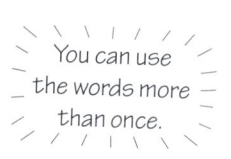

You can use the words more than once.

Use the words below to complete the paragraph about why they should do this.

| mouth | microorganisms | patient | disease | eyes | nose | hospital | cells |

Hand-washing reduces the risk of the doctors transferring .... from patients to their ...., ... and .... These parts of the body are where .... could enter and cause .... It also stops them being transferred from doctor to patient and from one .... to another. Wearing gloves will stop .... in the patient's blood getting into any cuts the doctor may have.

Q5 When cooking **chicken** it is important to take **precautions** to prevent **food poisoning**. Complete the table below to show what precautions you should take and why they are necessary (some have been done for you).

Precaution	Why it is necessary
	Stops pathogens from your hands getting on the chicken.
Cook the chicken thoroughly.	
	Stops pathogens from the raw chicken being transferred to your body or other food.
Disinfect the worktop after preparing the chicken.	

Top Tips: Make sure you know all the different ways we can reduce the chance of being exposed to pathogens. You should be doing some of these every day anyway, like practising good personal hygiene. I doubt you get the opportunity to sterilise surgical equipment very often though.

Section 2.2 — Humans as Living Organisms

The Body Fighting Off Disease

Q1 Sally is a **medical student** studying the ways that the body can **prevent** microorganisms **entering**.

a) Complete the passage using some of the words given in the box.

| platelets | cells | clot | microorganisms | antibodies |

The skin acts as a barrier to infection. If the skin is broken, e.g. if it is cut, ... can get into the body. ...., which are small fragments of ...., help the blood ...., which seals the wound and prevents infection.

b) Give two features, apart from skin, that can act as a barrier against pathogens.

1. ....

2. ....

Q2 Sophie is an **immunologist**. She studies how the body destroys different pathogens that enter it.

a) Circle the correct word(s) in each pair to complete each sentence below.

i) The **circulatory** / **immune** system attacks microorganisms in the body.

ii) The **white blood cells** / **platelets** in the body attack microorganisms.

b) Number the following sentences in the correct order to show how the body can attack an invading pathogen.

☐ The antibodies lock on to the antigens and cause the death of the pathogens.

☐ The white blood cells recognise a foreign antigen.

☐ White blood cells produce antibodies specific to the antigens of the pathogen.

☐ If the person is infected with the same pathogen again, the white blood cells will produce antibodies very quickly to prevent the person from getting ill.

c) HIV attacks white blood cells. Suggest how this could affect people with HIV.

....

....

Think about what the white blood cells in your body do.

Section 2.2 — Humans as Living Organisms

Immunisation

Q1 Melissa has just had a baby girl called Josie. The doctor has advised her that Josie should be **immunised** against certain diseases.

a) The doctor suggests to Melissa that Josie be immunised against **rubella**. Explain why girls are especially encouraged to be immunised against rubella.

....

....

b) Give **three** other diseases that the Doctor might suggest Josie is immunised against.

1. ....
2. ....
3. ....

c) Melissa wants to know **why** the immunisations are necessary. Fill in the gaps in the paragraph below using words from the box.

microorganism	white blood cells	immunised
antibodies	ill	immune

In the time it takes for the .... to make .... some microorganisms can make you very .... You can be .... against some diseases so that you become .... to that disease even though you've only ever encountered a dead or weakened form of the ....

d) Tick the boxes next to statements that are **advantages** of vaccination.

☐ If a high percentage of people are vaccinated against a disease, fewer unvaccinated people will catch it because there are fewer people with the disease to catch it from.

☐ Trained health workers are needed to administer vaccines.

☐ The fewer people that get ill, the lower the cost of treatment to hospitals.

Top Tips: Vaccinations are pretty brilliant really. You get given a few injections when you're young and it stops you getting all sorts of horrible diseases. Vaccinations help control loads of diseases that were once common and some diseases have almost been completely wiped out.

Section 2.2 — Humans as Living Organisms

Immunisation

Q2 Scientists developed a new **vaccine** against **virus Z**. **Twenty people** took part in a **trial** of the vaccine. The results of the trial are shown in the table.

Number of people who became immune to virus Z	18
Number of people who contracted the illness in the next year	1
Number of people who suffered side effects	7

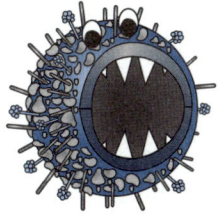

a) Give **two** disadvantages of the new vaccine.

1. ....

2. ....

b) What is the **advantage** of having a vaccine against virus Z? Tick the correct box.

Everybody who had the vaccine was immune to virus Z ☐

People who have the vaccine are less likely to get virus Z. ☐

The vaccine makes people immune to all other viruses. ☐

c) What percentage of participants in the trial **became immune** to the virus?

....

d) The following statements describe how the vaccine against virus Z works but they are in the wrong order. Put numbers in the boxes to show the correct order.

☐ The inactive virus Z microorganisms carry antigens so the white blood cells make antibodies against them.

☐ Antibodies are made very quickly and the virus Z microorganisms are killed before they have a chance to make you ill.

☐ If virus Z enters the body again, the white blood cells recognise it straight away.

☐ Inactive virus Z is injected into the body.

Section 2.2 — Humans as Living Organisms

Immunisation

Q3 The table shows the number of **cases** of **Disease X** reported in a country between 1982-2002. The graph shows the **uptake of the vaccine** used to prevent Disease X.

a) Plot the data displayed in the table on the graph below.

Year	Number of cases
1982	7600
1986	7500
1990	7200
1994	6650
1998	6100
2002	5100

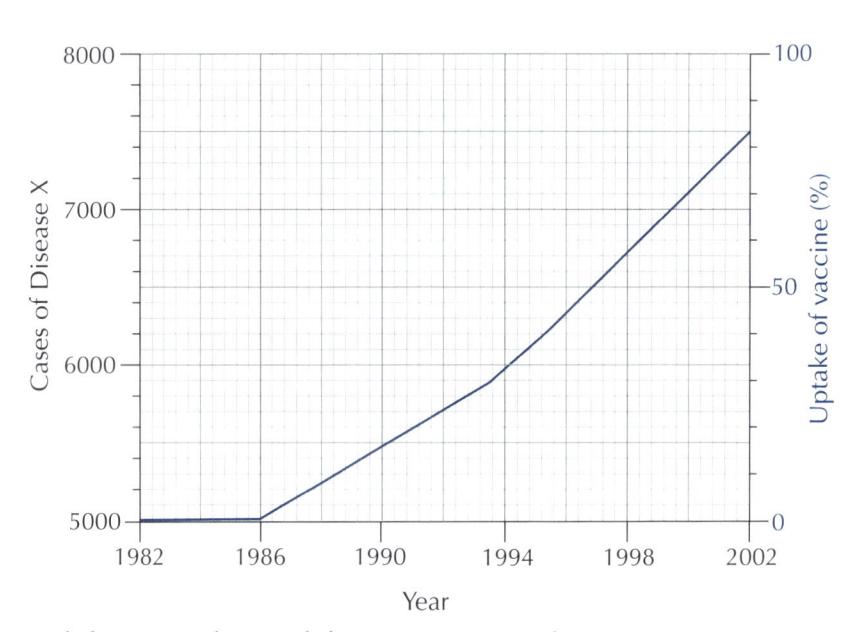

b) Describe and explain the trend shown on the graph between 1982 and 2002.

....

....

....

c) Which year was the vaccine introduced? ....

d) Approximately how many cases of Disease X were there in 1996? ....

e) The bar chart shows the number of cases of Disease X in different areas of the country in 2005.

   i) In which area are most cases of Disease X found?

   ....

   ii) Suggest a reason why this area has the highest number of cases.

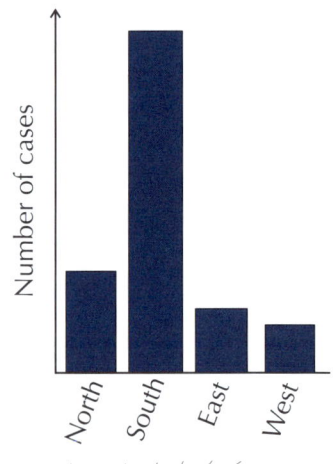

   ....

   ....

   ....

Think about what conditions increase the spread of disease.

Section 2.2 — Humans as Living Organisms

Use of Drugs to Treat Disease

Q1 Mohan is a **pharmacist**. He dispenses drugs, e.g. antibiotics, to people who are unwell.

a) State what type of organism the following drugs would be used to treat.

i) Antivirals

....

ii) Antibiotics

....

b) Why would antibiotics not be given to treat a cold?

....

....

c) Ringworm is a fungal infection. What type of drugs would be given to treat such an infection?

....

Q2 Dr Hamilton works in a **hospital**. She assesses patients and gives them the appropriate treatment.

a) Tick the boxes to indicate whether Dr Hamilton should give antibiotics, antivirals or antifungals to patients with the following diseases.

	antibiotics	antifungals	antivirals
i) **Athlete's foot** — a common fungal infection.	☐	☐	☐
ii) **Tuberculosis** — a bacterial lung infection.	☐	☐	☐
iii) **Meningitis** — swelling of tissue around the brain, which can be caused by bacteria.	☐	☐	☐
iv) **AIDS** — a disease caused by a virus (HIV).	☐	☐	☐
v) **Cholera** — a bacterial disease spread in water.	☐	☐	☐

b) What is the natural source of antibiotics?

....

c) Who **discovered** the first antibiotic?

....

Top Tips: The first ever antibiotic, penicillin, was discovered in 1928. Since then antibiotics have been widely used to treat all kinds of bacterial infections, saving loads of lives. All this is due to a forgetful scientist letting his experiments go mouldy. Pretty lucky really.

Section 2.2 — Humans as Living Organisms

Use of Drugs to Treat Disease

Q3 Ushma is a **technician** who works for a pharmaceutical company. She is involved in **testing new antibiotics** that are being developed by the company.

a) Why is it necessary for drugs to be tested before they can be sold and used by the public?

....

b) Number the following in the correct order to show the usual development and testing process for new drugs.

☐ Live animals

☐ Human volunteers

☐ Computer models

☐ Human tissue

c) Give one reason why computer models are often used when developing drugs.

....

....

d) Tick the boxes to show whether the statements are **true** or **false**.

	True	False
i) Human tissue can be used to test the effect of the drug on a whole body system.	☐	☐
ii) In the UK, new drugs must be tested on two different live mammals.	☐	☐
iii) A placebo contains the new medicine being tested.	☐	☐

e) Fill in the gaps in the paragraph below

| side effects | small | healthy | large | control | placebo | animals |

A clinical trial takes place after the drug has been tested on .... In the first stage the drug is tested on .... human volunteers, to determine if the drug has any .... If the results from the first stage are good, the drug is then tested on a .... number of patients and then a .... number of patients. At each stage of the clinical trial a .... group is given a dummy that does not contain the active drug being tested. This dummy is called a ....

Top Tips: It takes years for a drug to reach the general public. This is because they have to go through loads of different stages of development and testing. And as you'll see on the next page, some of the stages of drug testing can be pretty controversial...

Section 2.2 — Humans as Living Organisms

Use of Drugs to Treat Disease

Q4 Read the extract below and answer the following questions.

> Animal-rights campaigners gathered in Corel Square today to demonstrate against the opening of Froggarts' new animal testing laboratory. This lab carries out the final tests of new drugs on animals to make sure they're safe before they're used in clinical trials on humans.
>
> I interviewed several of the animal-rights campaigners, who made their grievances with the company very clear, saying, "Animals are so different from humans that testing on them is pointless", "Why should animals suffer for our benefit?" and "Animal testing shouldn't be used because it has failed to highlight the harmful side effects of some drugs".
>
> Despite these arguments, voiced by many pressure groups, the law states that 'finished' drugs must be tested on animals before they can be regarded as suitable for human trials.
>
> The head of scientific research at Froggarts pointed out that, "We share over 90% of our DNA with other primates and many other animals have very similar organs to our own, making them good models of the human body". However, he admitted that, "An extremely small number of side effects that humans experience cannot be detected in other organisms, but animal testing is still the safest way to make sure a drug isn't harmful to humans".
>
> In 2005, 395 000 animals were used for safety experiments in the UK. Of these animals, 73% were used for testing the safety of drugs. There are several laws in place to ensure that any pain caused by testing is kept to a minimum. These laws make UK testing regulations amongst the strictest in the world.
>
> The benefits of testing on animals are clear when you consider the millions of people whose lives have been improved by these drugs. For example, approximately 35 000 people are treated for breast cancer every year with drugs that have been tested on animals.
>
> Testing drugs on animals has been a highly controversial issue for decades. Without a realistic alternative in view, it will remain so for the foreseeable future.

a) How many animals were used for safety experiments in 2005?

....

b) Give **two** reasons why the animal-rights campaigners object to testing new medicines on live animals.

1. ....

2. ....

c) In your own words, explain why the head of scientific research at Froggarts still thinks that animals are good models to show how a new drug may work in humans.

....

....

Section 2.2 — Humans as Living Organisms

Recreational Drugs

Q1 A **drug counsellor** is telling the children at a local school about **solvents**.

a) Give **three** examples of useful substances that contain potentially dangerous solvents.

....

b) Use some of the words in the box to fill in the gaps and complete the passage.

| breathing | lungs | memory |
| decreasing | brain damage | eyes |

Solvents affect the nervous system by .... the speed at which messages are passed along neurones. Long-term solvent abuse often causes .... — symptoms of which include personality changes, trouble sleeping or loss of .... Solvents also damage the .... and can cause .... difficulties. Solvents can even kill, and this can happen the very first time you use them.

Q2 **Cannabis** is an **illegal** drug, but some scientists believe it can relieve the pain caused by some **chronic diseases**.

a) Give one example of a chronic disease for which there is evidence in favour of cannabis as a useful painkiller.

....

b) Name another type of misused drug that is a source of medicinal drugs.

....

Q3 A **doctor** is explaining to one of his patients the dangers of **alcohol abuse**.

a) What effect does long-term alcohol abuse have on the **brain**?

....

b) Describe the effect of excessive alcohol intake on the **liver**.

....

Section 2.2 — Humans as Living Organisms

Recreational Drugs

Q4 The graphs below show the number of **deaths** due to **heart disease** and **lung cancer** for **smokers** and **non-smokers** from a study of a group of 100 000 men.

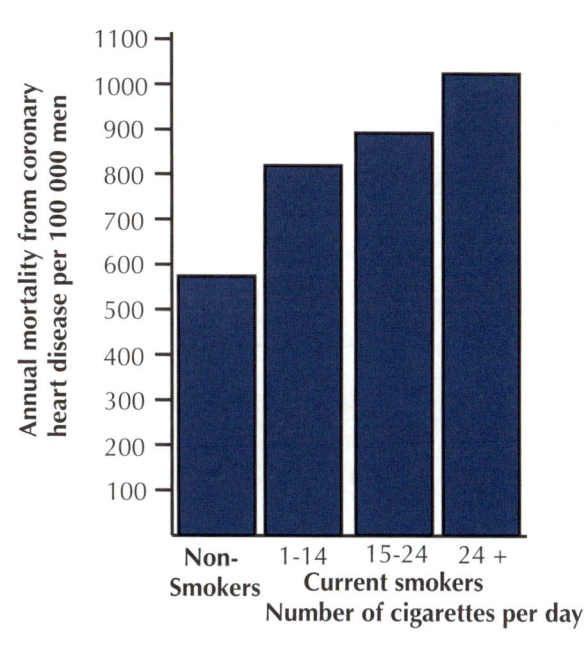

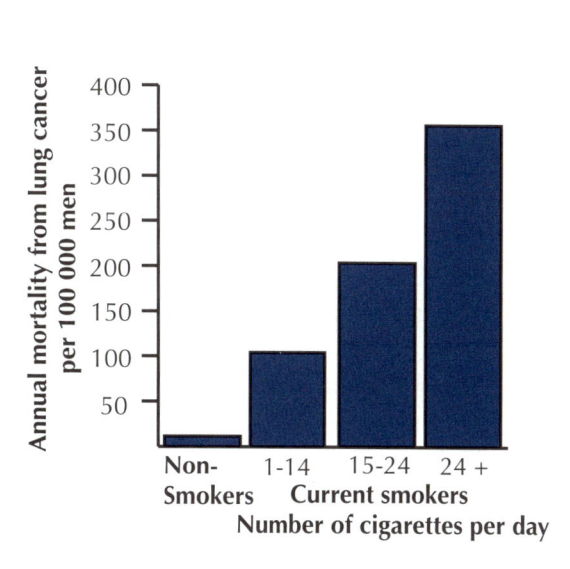

a) Approximately how many more deaths from coronary heart disease were there in smokers who smoke 1-14 cigarettes a day than in non-smokers?

.... per year per 100 000 men.

b) What is the difference between the number of lung cancer deaths in men smoking 15-24 cigarettes a day and men smoking more than 24 cigarettes a day? Circle the correct answer.

150   400   50   15

c) Describe the trend shown in the graph between smoking and heart disease.

....

....

d) Suggest another group of people that it would have been helpful to include in the study. Give a reason for your answer.

....

....

Think about who wasn't tested in the study.

e) Circle the name of the chemicals that are present in tobacco smoke that can cause cancer.

emphysema   carcinogens   barbiturates   amphetamines

f) What chemical in cigarettes makes smoking addictive?

....

Section 2.2 — Humans as Living Organisms

Recreational Drugs

Q5 Andy is a teacher. He's teaching some of his students about the effects of **smoking** on **health**.

a) Circle the correct word(s) in each pair to complete the paragraph below describing the effects of smoking on the circulatory system.

> Cigarette smoke contains carbon monoxide, which can combine with the **red** / **white** blood cells. This means that the blood can carry **less** / **more** oxygen. Smoking also causes disease of the **stomach** / **heart** and blood vessels. This can lead to **heart attacks** / **emphysema** and **cancer** / **strokes**.

b) Explain how an unborn baby can be affected if the mother smokes when pregnant.

....

....

c) Why have some countries banned smoking in public places such as bars and restaurants?

.... *Think about passive smoking.*

....

d) Smoking can cause respiratory diseases, e.g. lung cancer.
Circle two other respiratory diseases that can be caused by smoking.

    strokes   **emphysema**   **bronchitis**   **carcinogens**

Q6 In the UK, the legal limit for alcohol in the blood when driving is **80 mg per 100 cm³**. The table shows the number of 'units' of alcohol in different drinks. One **unit** increases the blood alcohol level by over **20 mg per 100 cm³** in most people.

DRINK	ALCOHOL UNITS
1 pint of strong lager	3
1 pint of beer	2
1 single measure of whisky	1

a) Bill drinks two pints of strong lager. How many units of alcohol has he had? ....

b) Is Bill's blood alcohol level likely to mean that he cannot legally drive? Explain your answer.

.... *Assume he drank the cans fairly quickly.*

....

c) Explain why it can be dangerous to drive a car after drinking alcohol.

....

Section 2.2 — Humans as Living Organisms

Genetic Disorders

Q1 Read the passage below and answer the following questions.

> Cystic fibrosis (CF) is one of the most common inherited diseases in the world. In Europe, 1 in 2500 children are born with this disorder, which affects the internal organs. The build up of sticky mucus in the lungs and digestive system, which the disease causes, can result in the sufferer having difficulty breathing and digesting food.
>
> Over 2 million people in the UK carry one faulty version of the gene that causes CF. However, CF only develops in individuals who have inherited a faulty gene from each parent.
>
> Cystic fibrosis currently affects over 7500 people in the UK. The condition is caused by a fault in a gene that helps to produce sweat, digestive juices and mucus, and can be diagnosed using genetic testing or a sweat test.
>
> As it's a genetic disorder there is no cure, but the CF gene has been identified and the symptoms can be treated with physiotherapy, medication and exercise. Scientists are currently researching the possibility of gene therapy as a treatment.
>
> Huntington's chorea is another genetic disorder, affecting between 5 and 8 people per 100 000. It is a neurological disorder affecting the brain. The gradual loss of brain function causes symptoms such as abnormal body movements (called chorea) and a lack of coordination. The disorder can also affect mental ability and some aspects of personality.
>
> Huntington's can develop in individuals who have inherited only one faulty gene from either parent. This means that a sufferer has a 50% chance of passing the disorder on to their children. The faulty gene affects the production of certain chemicals in the brain, causing damage to nerve cells in the brain. Huntington's currently affects around 4800 people in the UK.
>
> There is no cure for this disorder, however medication can be used to treat some physical and emotional symptoms. Nutrition is seen as an important part of treatment as sufferers usually need two or three times as many calories than the average person to maintain body weight.

a) How many people in the **UK** are currently suffering with cystic fibrosis?

....

b) Which genetic disorder, cystic fibrosis or Huntington's, is **more common**?

....

c) How are these disorders passed from person to person?

....

d) On average, how many more **calories** does a Huntington's sufferer need to maintain body weight, compared to a non-sufferer?

....

e) Lou suffers from Huntington's chorea. If he decides to have children with a non-sufferer what is the chance that he will pass the condition on to his children?

....

Section 2.2 — Humans as Living Organisms

Mixed Questions for Sections 2.1 and 2.2

Q1 Lance farms his land **intensively** but he's thinking of changing to **organic** farming. Lance must take a lot of factors into account when making this decision.

a) Lance uses artificial fertilisers on his crops to make sure they have all the **minerals** they need. State why plants need each of the following minerals.

i) Nitrates ....

ii) Magnesium ....

b) **Organic** farmers must follow different **guidelines** from those followed by **intensive** farmers. Tick the boxes to show whether the following statements apply to organic or intensive farms.

                                                                                                      Organic Intensive

i) Artificial fertilisers are used. ☐ ☐

ii) Weeding is carried out by hand. ☐ ☐

iii) Animals are free to roam outside for a set time. ☐ ☐

iv) Artificial pesticides and herbicides are used. ☐ ☐

c) Food produced by organic farmers is **increasing** in popularity even though it tends to be more expensive than food produced intensively.

i) Suggest a reason why organically produced food is increasing in **popularity**.

....

ii) Why might this change as the world's population continues to **increase**?

Think about which farming method can produce more food.

....

....

Q2 **All** living things, including humans and plants, **respire**.

a) Fill in the word equation for respiration using some of the words given.

    oxygen   carbon dioxide   nitrogen   water   glucose   energy   chlorophyll

.... + ... → .... + ...

(+ ....)

b) Respiration **requires** glucose. Plants and humans obtain glucose in **different** ways.

i) What is the **process** called by which plants make glucose? ....

ii) Humans obtain glucose by eating plants and animals. Number the boxes to describe how glucose is obtained from food.

☐ Glucose moves from the digestive system into the blood.

☐ Food is digested into glucose.

☐ The blood carries the glucose to the cells.

☐ Sugary food is eaten.

Mixed Questions for Sections 2.1 and 2.2

Q3 Jane felt constantly thirsty and tired so she went to see her **doctor**. He told her she might be suffering from **diabetes**.

a) What is the name of the **organ** that produces insulin? ....

b) Circle the correct word from each pair to complete the following paragraph on insulin.

> The pancreas / liver detects an increase in blood glucose levels and releases insulin / glucose. Glucose is then removed from the blood by the liver / pancreas.

c) The doctor tells Jane that diabetes can be **controlled** in two ways.
Tick the **two** correct answers.

- ☐ Eating lots of food rich in carbohydrate.
- ☐ Avoiding foods rich in carbohydrate.
- ☐ Injecting glucose.
- ☐ Injecting insulin.

d) Jane's dad works for a **pharmaceutical company**. His company have **genetically modified** a pig to produce human insulin.

i) What has been **transferred** into the pig's cells to make it genetically engineered? ....

ii) Some people think genetic engineering is wrong.
Give **one** advantage and **one** risk of genetically engineering animals.

Advantage ....

Risk ....

Q4 Nasser is feeling **ill** and thinks that he must have an **infection**. He goes to see a doctor.

a) The doctor tells Nasser that he has **influenza**, which is a viral infection.
Name **two** other illnesses caused by viruses.

1. .... 2. ....

b) Give **two** ways that white blood cells respond to viruses and other pathogens entering the body.

1. ....

2. ....

c) How could Nasser have **reduced** his chances of being infected with influenza?

....

....

Mixed Questions for Sections 2.1 and 2.2

Q5 Dr Brooks works in a **hospital**. A patient comes in with a suspected case of **tuberculosis** (TB).

a) i) Draw lines to link the following diseases with the drugs used to treat them.

Tuberculosis   Antifungal

Athlete's foot   Antiviral

Measles   Antibiotic

ii) What type of organism can produce **antibiotics**? ....

b) Dr Brooks checked the patient's medical records and found that she was never **immunised** against TB. Fill in the blanks with the words given to complete the paragraph below.

killed   antibodies   live   harmless   weakened   specific

Immunisation involves injecting dead or .... microorganisms into the body. These microorganisms are .... but still carry antigens. .... are made by the body to attack the microorganisms. If .... microorganisms then enter the body they can be .... immediately as the body can make .... antibodies against that microorganism very quickly.

Q6 Akemi is a **dairy farmer** at Froggarts Farm. He looks after a herd of cows that have been **selectively bred**. Three of his cows are ill with an **infection**.

a) Suggest **two** desirable characteristics Akemi's cows may have been selectively bred for.

1. ....

2. ....

b) Why might Akemi's herd have **problems** with this infection? Tick the correct answer.

☐ Producing higher milk yields makes the cows more likely to get ill.

☐ Dairy cows are more likely to get ill than cows bred for meat.

☐ They have a reduced gene pool so there's less chance of resistance being present in the herd.

c) Akemi's suspects the infection is caused by a **virus**.
Give **one** example of an infection caused by a virus in **animals**. ....

d) How could Akemi **reduce** the chance of the new disease spreading?

....

Section 2.3 — Obtaining Useful Chemicals

Classifying Chemicals

Q1 Tick the boxes to show whether the statements are **true** or **false**.

		True	False
a)	Elements contain only one type of atom.	☐	☐
b)	Mixtures contain different types of atoms bonded together chemically.	☐	☐
c)	Mixtures are easier to separate than compounds.	☐	☐

Q2 The picture below shows Julie making a cup of coffee. Six items are labelled — two of these are **elements**, two are **compounds** and two are **mixtures**.

Steel is made of iron and copper atoms that are not chemically bonded together.

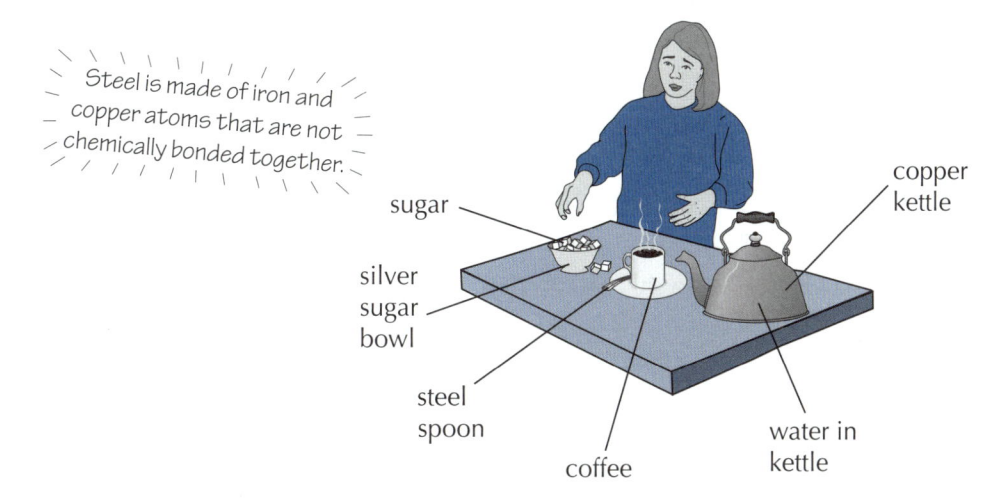

Labels: sugar, silver sugar bowl, steel spoon, coffee, water in kettle, copper kettle

a) The two elements are .... and ....

b) The two compounds are .... and ....

c) The two mixtures are .... and ....

Q3 Farouk has drawn diagrams to represent **elements**, **compounds** and **mixtures**. Match the letter of each diagram to the types of substances given.

A, B, 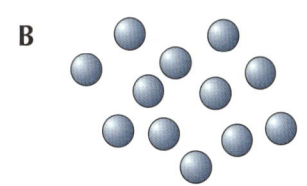 C, 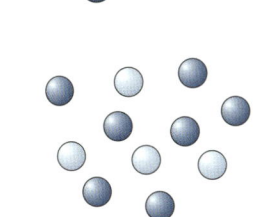 D

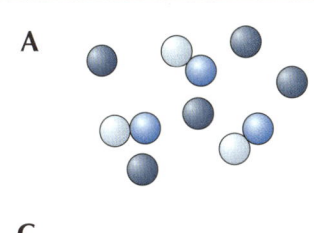

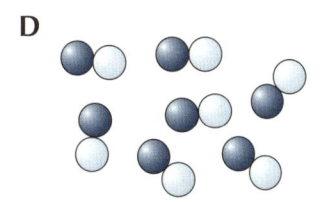

a) Element .... b) Compound ....

c) Mixture of elements .... d) Mixture of elements and compounds ....

Chemical Symbols and Notation

Q1 Draw lines to connect each element with its chemical symbol.

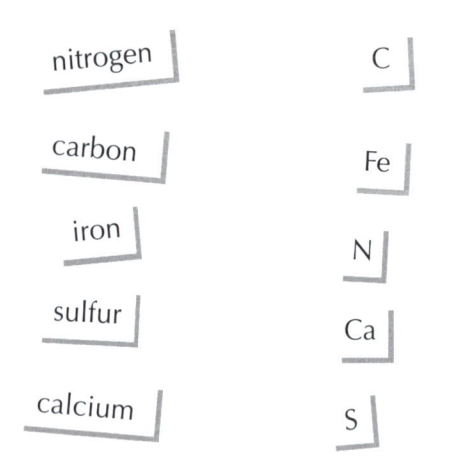

nitrogen — C
carbon — Fe
iron — N
sulfur — Ca
calcium — S

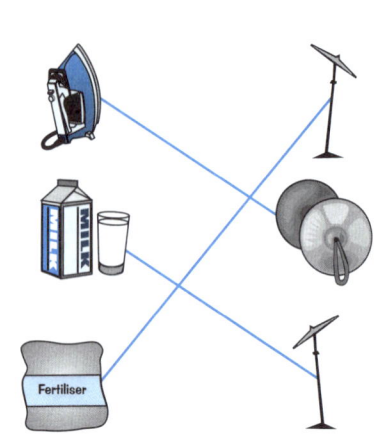

Q2 Laurence has a part-time job helping Professor Bumble in his **laboratory**. The professor gives Laurence a list chemical symbols to brush up on, but Laurence spills his coffee over the **list**.

a) Complete the table with the missing elements and chemical symbols from Professor Bumble's list and tick the correct box to show whether the element is a metal or non-metal.

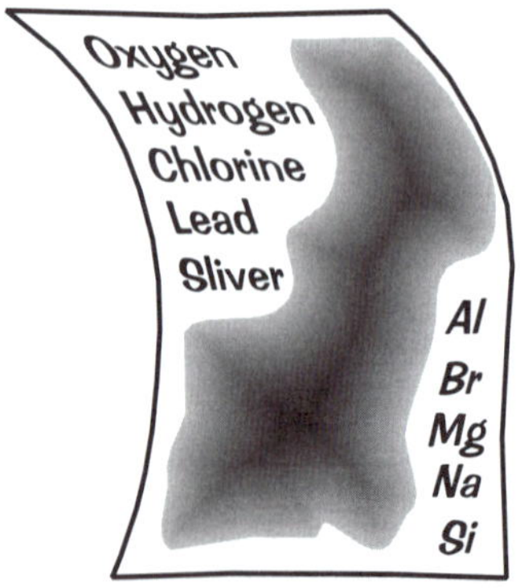

Element	Chemical symbol	Metal	Non-metal
Oxygen			✓
Hydrogen			
Chlorine			
Lead			
Silver			
	Al		
	Br		
	Mg		
	Na		
	Si		

b) i) The professor asks Laurence to get some zinc, phosphorus and barium from the cupboard. When Laurence gets there the containers only have the chemical symbols on them, not their names. Write the chemical symbols for zinc, phosphorus and barium.

Zinc ....   Phosphorus ....   Barium ....

ii) Laurence sees the following symbols on some other containers. Write down what they contain.

F ....   K ....

Section 2.3 — Obtaining Useful Chemicals

Chemical Building Blocks

Q1 Draw lines to match up each word below with the statement that best describes it.

- Electrons — These are found in the nucleus along with protons.
- Protons — The atomic number is the number of these in an element.
- Atoms — These move around the nucleus in shells.
- Neutrons — These are what all matter is made up of.

Q2 George is a **scuba diving** instructor. When he goes diving he takes a bottle of **oxygen** so that he can breathe underwater.

Uh-oh, looks like I brought the helium bottle again!

Label this diagram of an oxygen atom.

a) ....

b) ....
  composed of ....
  and ....

Q3 Fill in the missing numbers of **protons** and **electrons** in the following atoms.

C — carbon: Protons 6, Electrons 6

H — hydrogen: Protons 1, Electrons 1

All atoms that make up a chemical element have the same number of protons and electrons.

O — oxygen: Protons 8, Electrons 8

N — nitrogen: Protons 7, Electrons 7

O: Protons ...., Electrons ....

C: Protons ...., Electrons ....

N: Protons ...., Electrons ....

H: Protons ...., Electrons ....

Section 2.3 — Obtaining Useful Chemicals

Compounds and Formulas

Q1 Simon is a **meteorologist**. Every day he produces a report on the **air quality** at the weather station where he works.

a) Write the names of the following compounds that Simon finds in an air sample.

i) CO_2 .... ii) H_2O ....

iii) CH_4 .... iv) NH_3 ....

b) Simon also monitors acid rain. One of the acids found in acid rain is dilute **sulfuric acid**.

i) One of the problems with acid rain is that it causes erosion to limestone buildings. The word equation for the reaction that occurs is shown below.

sulfuric acid + calcium carbonate → carbon dioxide + calcium sulfate + water

Complete the symbol equation for the reaction. It is already balanced.

.... + ... → .... + $CaSO_4$ + ...

ii) Complete the following sentence by circling the correct word in each pair.

In the reaction above, everything on the left hand side of the equation is a **product** / **reactant**, and everything on the right hand side is a **product** / **reactant**.

Q2 Draw lines to match up the **compounds** below to their **formulas**. Two have been done for you.

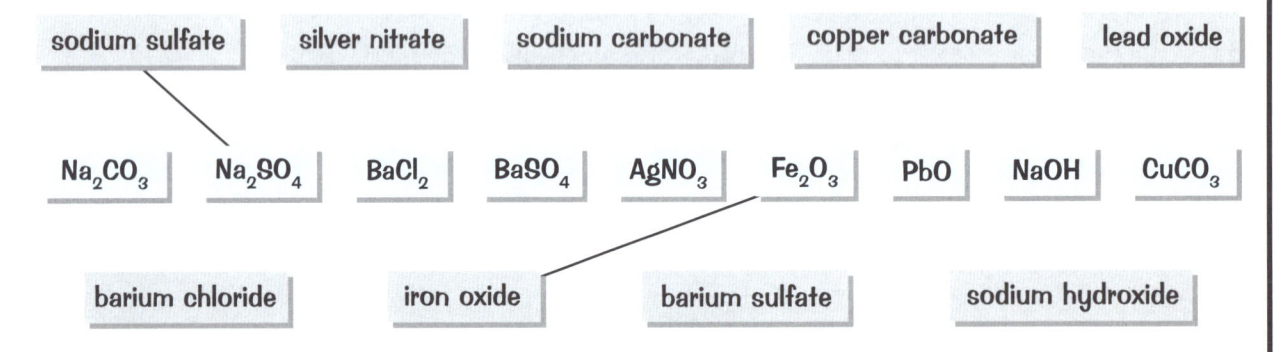

sodium sulfate   silver nitrate   sodium carbonate   copper carbonate   lead oxide

Na_2CO_3 Na_2SO_4 $BaCl_2$ $BaSO_4$ $AgNO_3$ Fe_2O_3 PbO $NaOH$ $CuCO_3$

barium chloride   iron oxide   barium sulfate   sodium hydroxide

Q3 Complete the table by filling in the missing names and formulas of the compounds.

Compound	Formula
	$CuSO_4$
potassium nitrate	
	$NaCl$
calcium oxide	
hydrochloric acid	

Section 2.3 — Obtaining Useful Chemicals

Organic and Inorganic Chemicals

Q1 Scientists classify chemicals into two broad categories — **organic** and **inorganic**.

a) Complete the following passage using words from the list below.
Each word can be used more than once.

inorganic	carbon	living	organic	non-living

Most compounds that contain the element .... are classed as

.... The word .... means 'derived from

.... matter' — all living things contain ....

.... compounds do not usually contain ....

— they come from .... sources.

b) Classify the chemicals below as organic or inorganic by putting them into the correct column in the table.

CuO C_2H_5OH $C_6H_{12}O_6$ K_2Si_4 Co C_6H_5OH

NaCl   Fe Al_2SiO_5 C_2H_4

Organic	Inorganic

Use the formulas to work out if they contain carbon.

c) Tick the boxes to show whether the following types of chemicals are organic or inorganic.

	Organic	Inorganic
i) metals	☐	☐
ii) ceramics	☐	☐
iii) artificial fertilisers	☐	☐
iv) polymers	☐	☐

Q2 **Fossil fuels are very useful and important in day to day life.**

Explain why fossil fuels are a good source of organic chemicals.

....

....

Section 2.3 — Obtaining Useful Chemicals

Useful Chemicals From Rocks

Q1 Jack is a **geologist** — he studies rocks and **compounds** that are extracted from the **ground**.

a) Complete the following passage using words from the list below.

mixed   compounds   non-metal   calcium   metal   carbonate   sulfate   uncombined

> Sulfur (a ....) and gold (a ....) are useful elements that are mined or quarried out of the ground. They are both usually found in an .... state, so can be used without the need for further processing. Limestone and marble are examples of the chemical compound .... They are mined or quarried and can also be used straight from the ground without the need for further processing.

b) Explain why substances such as gold and sulfur can be used straight from the ground.

....

....

Q2 List two uses for **sulfur**, **gold**, **limestone** and **marble**.

a) Sulfur
1. ....
2. ....

b) Gold
1. ....
2. ....

c) Limestone
1. ....
2. ....

Think about how limestone is used in the building industry.

d) Marble
1. ....
2. ....

Top Tips: It's been known for thousands of years that limestone is a dead useful building material. The Greeks used it to make sarcophaguses, Romans used to use it to build things like aqueducts and today we crush it up to make roads — bet those Romans are turning in their graves.

Section 2.3 — Obtaining Useful Chemicals

Useful Chemicals From Rocks

Q3 Mr Adid is a science teacher. He wants to do a **laboratory** experiment to demonstrate how **salt** is separated from **rock salt**.

a) Put the stages of the experiment into the correct order by putting numbers in the boxes.

☐ Leave until all the water has evaporated to give salt crystals.

☐ Filter the mixture to remove the sand.

☐ Grind up the rock salt, put it into a container and add water.

☐ Heat gently, stirring all the time, until all the salt has dissolved.

b) The method used in the **laboratory** differs to that used in **industry**. Complete the following passage using words from the list below to describe the method used in industry.

| chloride | vacuum | dissolved | brine | crushed | sodium | filtered | impurities | kiln |

First, chunks of rock salt are .... using a machine and then .... in water to form .... This is .... and chemicals are added to remove .... in the solution. A piece of equipment called a .... evaporator is used to produce pure crystals of ...., which are then dried in a ....

Q4 Salt, **sodium chloride**, has many uses.

a) Complete the following sentence by circling the correct word below.

Rock salt is an example of an element / a mixture / a compound obtained from the Earth's crust.

b) Apart from salt, what other substance is found in rock salt?

....

c) Give one use of rock salt in its **unpurified** form.

....

d) Give two uses of salt in its **purified** form.

1. ....

2. ....

Section 2.3 — Obtaining Useful Chemicals

Useful Chemicals From Rocks

Q5 Gillian is a **petrochemical scientist** who works for an **oil company**. She has been asked to give a presentation to school children to explain **how** and **why oil is refined**.

a) The notes Gillian prepared for her presentation have been dropped and jumbled up. Write numbers in the boxes to show the correct order of the sentences.

A The different fractions in the crude oil condense at different temperatures. ☐

B Crude oil is formed from the buried remains of animals and plants. It is extracted from the ground by drilling. ☐

C The different chemicals are collected from different parts of the column — the bottom of the column is the hottest, and the top of the column is coolest. The different chemicals are used for different things. ☐

D The crude oil is heated until it evaporates, and the vapours rise up the column. ☐

b) What is the name of the **process** that separates crude oil into more useful substances?

....

c) Name **six** substances that are produced by this process.

1. ....   4. ....
2. ....   5. ....
3. ....   6. ....

Q6 Some scientists believe that the supply of **crude oil** will run out within the next **fifty years**. The table below shows some products crude oil is used to make.

Product	Currently made from	Alternatives to using crude oil
Fuels	Crude oil	Wind / solar / nuclear
Drugs	Crude oil	None
Paints	Crude oil	Plant oils

a) Explain why some people think that we should stop using crude oil to make fuels and just use it to make things like drugs.

....

....

b) Give two other **consumer products**, other than those listed in the table, that are made from the chemicals in crude oil.

1. ....   2. ....

Section 2.3 — Obtaining Useful Chemicals

Extracting Metals From Rocks

Q1 What is a **metal ore**?

....

....

Q2 Emilio works for a large **mining** company, which also **extracts metals** from their **ores**. He is learning about the different methods used by the company.

a) Use words from the list below to complete the following passage.

| compounds | reactive | lead | extracted | iron |

Most chemical substances are found in the Earth as compounds and are in mixtures that require separation. Metals such as .... and .... occur naturally as .... because they are .... These metals need to be .... using chemical methods.

b) Describe how **iron** can be extracted from **iron ore**.

....

c) Write a word equation for the extraction of iron from iron(III) oxide.

....

Q3 **Scientists** have developed several ways to **minimise** the effect of **metal extraction** on the **environment**.

a) One way is to use **gas scrubbing**. Suggest how this process produces less pollution.

....

....

b) Give two other examples of methods used to reduce the amount of pollution created by metal extraction.

1. ....

2. ....

Section 2.3 — Obtaining Useful Chemicals

Extracting Metals From Rocks

Q4 The Keegan brothers run a large **tin mine**.
The table on the right shows their annual spending.

Keegan Bros Mine Annual expenditure	
Cost	£ (thousands)
Transport	20
Machinery	35
Electricity	1.5
Labour	63
Metal refining	
Total	131.5

a) Use the table to answer the questions below.

   i) How much is spent on 'Metal refining'?
   Circle the correct answer.

   £12 000   £15 000   £20 000

   ii) What is the quarry's biggest expense?
   ....

   iii) What percentage of the total cost is spent on machinery?
   ....

b) Mining causes **environmental problems**.

   i) A large amount of **waste rock** is produced by the mine. This has to be transported to a separate site, two and a half miles away. Explain how this could damage the environment.
   ....
   ....

   ii) Describe the effect mining can have on the **landscape**.
   ....
   ....

   iii) What effect does mining have on plants and animals in the surrounding area?
   ....
   ....

c) Profits from the mine have been falling over recent years and so the Keegan brothers plan to close it. Give **two** potential disadvantages that closing the mine might cause for the local town.

   1. ....
   2. ....

Top Tips: Metals are much more useful after they've been extracted from their ores. Make sure that you understand how a metal oxide can be reduced. It's also an idea to learn why extracting metals can be bad for the environment and how these problems can be reduced.

Section 2.3 — Obtaining Useful Chemicals

Industrial Production of Chemicals

Q1 The **chemical industry** is responsible for manufacturing products that we use every day. Raw materials are used to produce **bulk** or **fine** chemicals.

a) Complete the following passage using words from the box below to describe the difference between fine chemicals and bulk chemicals.

specialist	medicines	fertilisers	small	large

Fine chemicals include chemicals such as ....
They're produced on a .... scale and require
.... production. Chemicals such as
.... require .... scale
production in the chemical industry — these chemicals are called
bulk chemicals.

b) Tick the boxes to show whether the products below are bulk chemicals or fine chemicals.

                Bulk Fine

i) Sulfuric acid ☐ ☐

ii) Medicine ☐ ☐

iii) Pigments ☐ ☐

iv) Ammonia ☐ ☐

v) Dyes ☐ ☐

vi) Poly(ethene) ☐ ☐

Q2 A **pharmaceuticals company** wants to speed up its **manufacturing process**. Scientists working for the company are investigating different ways of making the **chemical reactions quicker**.

Give four ways that scientists can speed up chemical reactions.

1. ....

2. ....

3. ....

4. ....

Don't just state the factors that speed up the rate of a chemical reaction — say how to increase the speed.

Section 2.3 — Obtaining Useful Chemicals

Industrial Production of Chemicals

Q3 Mike is the manager of a **chemical company** that produces **cleaning products**. He employs a wide range of people with different **skills**.

a) Gwen is a **research scientist** in Mike's company. Suggest what might her job involve.

....

....

b) Some of the manufacturing processes used by the company cause **pollution**. Mike wants to employ someone to help minimise this. What field should this employee be an expert in?

....

c) Gary works in the **quality control** department. Suggest what his role might involve.

....

....

d) One of the employees, Brian, is responsible for **refining** the **manufacturing process** — his job to make sure the processes are safe, efficient and profitable.

The table below outlines four different processes (A, B, C and D) that could be used to make a new floor polish — 'In the Buff'.

Process	Raw materials cost (£m)	Running costs (£m)	Level of pollution created	Product (tonnes)
A	10	11	High	550
B	5	11	Moderate	600
C	21	7	Moderate	480
D	13	9	High	520

i) Which process has the highest **initial costs** (the cost of the raw materials and running costs)?

....

ii) What other costs might be incurred during the process?

....

iii) Which process should Brian choose? Give reasons for your answer.

....

....

Section 2.3 — Obtaining Useful Chemicals

Industrial Production of Chemicals

Q4 Rachel works for a company that produces a range of industrial chemicals. She is investigating what affects the **rate of the reactions** involved.

Reaction A is carried out under normal conditions. Reaction B has been modified in some way.

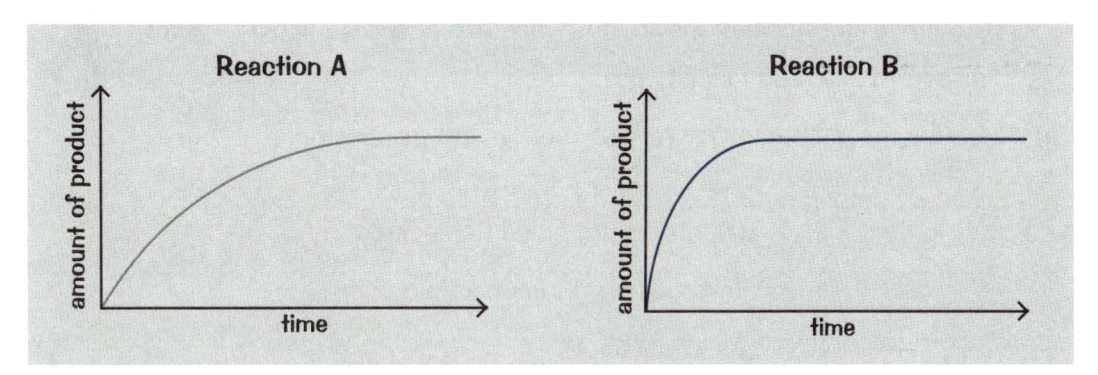

a) Which reaction (A or B) is **faster**? Explain your answer.

....

b) One of Rachel's colleagues, Alex, says that reaction B produces the **most product**. Is he right? Explain your answer.

....

....

c) Changing the **temperature** at which the reaction is carried out can affect the rate of reaction. Suggest what might happen to the rate of reaction A if the temperature was lowered.

....

d) Other than changing the temperature, suggest one way Rachel could change the rate of the reaction.

....

e) Complete the following passage using words in the box.

| cost | compromise | increase | slow | speed | fuel | low | high |

When reactions are carried out at a .... temperature the rate is too

.... To .... the rate, the temperature can be increased.

But, if the temperature is raised too much then the amount of energy used will increase and

.... costs will be too .... For this reason it is important

to reach a .... between factors such as ...., reaction

..............................., safety and environmental issues.

Section 2.3 — Obtaining Useful Chemicals

Useful Mixtures

Q1 When **chemists** design new products they choose the **type of mixture** according to what the product will be **used** for.

a) i) Complete the following sentence by circling the correct words.

Solutions and suspensions are both mixtures of **solids** / **liquids** / **gases** dispersed in a **solid** / **liquid** / **gas**.

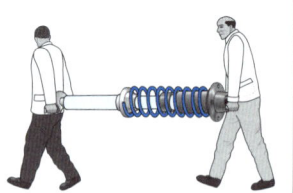

ii) Describe the difference between a solution and suspension.

....

....

....

iii) Give an example of a:

solution .... suspension ....

b) i) Complete the passage below using words in the box.

solid	dispersed	liquid	continuous	particles	gas

Colloids consist of small .... of one substance finely dispersed in another substance. The particles are the .... phase and can be a ...., ... or .... The liquid that contains the particles is called the .... phase.

ii) Why don't colloids separate out?

....

Q2 Kiran has prepared some mixtures for testing. Unfortunately he has to leave them for half an hour and when he comes back, some of them look different. Use the before and after pictures below to decide what **type of mixtures** they could be.

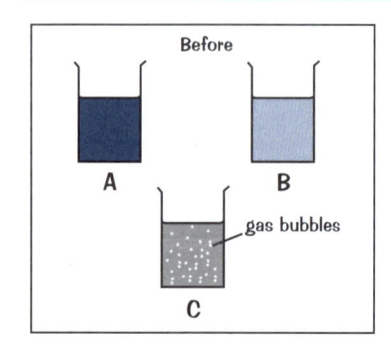

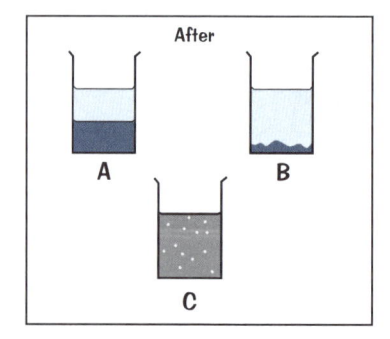

A ....
B ....
C ....

Section 2.4 — Chemical and Material Behaviour

Useful Mixtures

Q3 Scientists working in the **cosmetics industry** often use different **colloids** such as **gels**, **aerosols** and **foams**.

a) i) Complete the following sentence by circling the correct words.

Gels are made from a solid / liquid / gas dispersed in a solid / liquid / gas.

ii) Give one use for a **gel** and explain how its properties make it suited to that use.

....

....

b) i) Which of the following are **aerosols**? Circle the correct answer(s).

shaving foam   hairspray   toothpaste   shower gel   spray paint

ii) Explain how the properties of aerosols make them suited to their uses.

....

....

c) i) Use words from the list below to complete the following sentence about **foams**.

continuous   liquid   solid   dispersed   gas

> Foams consist of tiny .... bubbles (the ....
> phase) dispersed in either a .... or ....
> (the .... phase).

ii) Give one use for a foam.

....

Q4 Jamal works in the **research and development** department of a large **paint** manufacturer. He is looking into the use of **emulsions** and **sols** for a new range of paints.

Complete the following sentences by circling the correct words.

> Paints made from sols consist of a mixture of small solid / liquid pigments dispersed in an oily solid / liquid base. Sols are well suited for use as paints because the solid can be applied as a liquid.
>
> Emulsion paints consist of tiny droplets of a solid / liquid dispersed in a solid / liquid, but they don't properly dissolve / evaporate in each other.
>
> Another common example of an emulsion is stained glass / mayonnaise.

Section 2.4 — Chemical and Material Behaviour

Chemical Bonding and Properties

Q1 Tick the boxes to show whether these statements are **true** or **false**.

True False

a) In ionic bonding, atoms lose or gain electrons. ☐ ☐

b) Ions with opposite charges repel each other. ☐ ☐

c) Ionic bonds always produce giant ionic structures. ☐ ☐

d) Ions in a giant ionic structure are loosely packed together. ☐ ☐

e) Ionic compounds dissolve to form solutions that conduct electricity. ☐ ☐

Q2 Sodium chloride (salt) has a **giant ionic structure**.

a) Circle the correct words to explain why sodium chloride has a **high melting point**.

> Salt has very **strong** / **weak** chemical bonds between the sodium ions and the chlorine ions. This means that it needs a **small** / **large** amount of energy to break the bonds when salt is melted.

b) Name two other **properties** of compounds with **giant ionic structures**.

1. ....

2. ....

Q3 Malcolm works for 'A Salt and Battery' — a company that makes **rechargeable batteries** for remote controlled cars, boats and planes. The batteries are made using lithium salts, which are **ionic compounds**.

a) Choose words from the box below to complete the following passage.

| negative | opposite | attracted | electrons | charged | neutrons |

> In ionic bonding atoms lose or gain .... to form .... particles. These are then strongly .... to one another because of the attraction of .... charges.

b) Why are most covalent compounds not suitable for using in batteries?

....

Top Tips: Compounds, both ionic and covalent, are formed when two or more elements chemically react together. The properties of the compound are completely different to the original elements. You need to know the characteristic properties of both types of compounds for the exam.

Section 2.4 — Chemical and Material Behaviour

Chemical Bonding and Properties

Q4 Fill in the blanks choosing from the words below to complete the following passage.

| giant | density | lattice | weak | lost | charged | electrons | dull |

Unlike solid ionic compounds, solid covalent compounds tend to have a .... appearance and low .... Covalent bonds form by sharing .... Many covalent compounds form small molecules with .... forces of attraction between the molecules. Some form structures with stronger bonds. In these structures the atoms are arranged in a regular .... — these are known as .... structures.

Q5 Draw lines to match the **properties** of covalent compounds on the left with their **causes** on the right.

Small molecules tend to have a low melting point.

Covalent compounds do not conduct electricity.

Giant covalent structures have a high melting point.

There are strong bonds between the ions.

Covalent compounds do not have free electrons.

There are weak forces of attraction between the molecules.

Q6 Ahmed is a materials scientist investigating four **covalent compounds** with different properties. **Sodium chloride** and **magnesium chloride** are used in cooking, while **silicon tetrachloride** and **phosphorus trichloride** are highly toxic industrial chemicals.

a) Explain why the chlorides of silicon and phosphorus have low melting points. Use the information in the table to help you.

....

....

Name	Structure	Melting point / °C
Sodium chloride	Giant ionic	801
Magnesium chloride	Giant ionic	714
Silicon tetrachloride	Small covalent	−70
Phosphorus trichloride	Small covalent	−112

b) Silica (silicon dioxide) has a melting point of 1710 °C. Explain why silica has such a high melting point.

Remember — silica has a giant covalent structure.

....

....

c) Ammonia (NH_3) has a melting point of -74 °C. Is its structure small or giant? ....

Section 2.4 — Chemical and Material Behaviour

Ceramics

Q1 Draw lines to match each ceramic with the material(s) from which it is made.

glass	limestone and clay
pottery and porcelain	sand and other chemicals
cement	clay

Q2 Walter is a salesman in a shop that specialises in bathroom suites. He is discussing the possibility of a new **ceramic bathroom** with some customers.

a) Give **two** properties of ceramics that make them suitable for use in bathrooms.

1. ....

2. ....

b) Give **one** reason why a metal might be a better choice for bathroom fittings.

....

c) Why do you think some people still prefer ceramics to metals?

....

Q3 Ceramics are commonly used for a number of **fixtures and fittings** around the home. Put ticks in the boxes below to show why the objects listed are made from ceramics.

You can tick more than one box for each object.

	Hard wearing — it doesn't scratch easily	Waterproof and smooth — it's easily cleaned and hygienic	High melting point — it's fire resistant	Inert — it doesn't corrode
Porcelain toilet				
Ceramic kitchen sink				
Brick fire place				
Glass coffee table				

Top Tips: Make sure you learn this stuff on ceramics inside out. You need to know examples of ceramics, like glass, cement and pottery. There could also be a question that asks about the properties of ceramics and why these properties make ceramics useful materials.

Section 2.4 — Chemical and Material Behaviour

Ceramics

Q4 John is teaching an evening class about the different **ceramics** used in the building industry and how they can be **made**. Use words from the box to complete the passage below.

| set | concrete | moulded | glazed | fired |

When clay is wet it can be .... into any shape. If it is then ....
into pottery or porcelain it will keep its shape. It can also be .... to add
colours or patterns. Other well known ceramics include glass and cement. Cement
becomes runny when mixed with water. It will eventually .... and harden.
It can also be used to make ....

Q5 Scientists are constantly researching ways of making glass that is **tougher** and easier to **clean**. Currently, plastics are cheaper than glass and break less easily.

Why do you think we still use glass for glazing rather than plastic?
....
....

Think about what happens to plastic safety goggles over time and how hard it is to see out of them.

Q6 Ben is designing a **TV** in his graphic design class. He'd like to use ceramics in his design.

a) Ben thought about using a ceramic like porcelain or pottery for the outer casing of the TV.

   i) Give two advantages of using a ceramic for this purpose.

   1. ....
   2. ....

   ii) Give one disadvantage of using a ceramic for this purpose.

   ....

b) Ben decided that his TV screen should be made out of glass.

   i) Give two reasons why glass is suited to this use.

   1. ....
   2. ....

   ii) Why do you think reinforced plastic is usually used instead of glass for hand-held TV screens?

   ....

Section 2.4 — Chemical and Material Behaviour

Polymers

Q1 Polymers have many uses in the modern world. Complete the passage about polymers and some of their uses with words from the box.

> electricity   poor   dense   shopping bags
> insulators   good   rigid   heat

Some polymers, e.g. polyethene, are very flexible. This property makes them good for .... and squeezy bottles. Polyethene wouldn't be suitable for making car bumpers though. A more .... polymer like polypropene is often used for this. Most polymers are .... conductors of .... and .... Because polymers are good .... they're often used to make casings for electrical appliances.

Q2 A chair designer is researching different polymers that could be used to make a new range of chairs.

Polymer	Flexibility
Polyethene	Very flexible
Polypropene	Not flexible, very rigid
Nylon	Flexible

a) Why would the designer not want to make chairs out of polyethene?

....

b) Which polymer do you think the designer should pick? Explain your choice.

....

Q3 Gladys sees an advert for a kettle in a magazine. The casing of the kettle is made from a polymer.

a) Which of the following polymers would be the most suitable for making the casing of the kettle? Circle the correct answer.

    nylon   melamine   poly(ethene)

b) Explain your answer to part a).

....

Section 2.4 — Chemical and Material Behaviour

Polymers

Q4 Felicity is a **material scientist** working for a company that produces a range of kitchen appliances and accessories. Complete the table by giving one **property** that the polymer used to make each object would need to have.

Use of polymer	Property the polymer would need
Spatula	
Work surface	
Frying pan handle	
Insulation around the electrical lead of a kettle	

Q5 Mark works in the **research and development** department of a large **electronics company**. He is currently looking into new materials with which to make the casing of a **laptop** computer. The table below shows some of the **properties** of four new polymers he could use.

Polymer	Density (g/cm³)	Strength	Flexibility	Price (£/kg)
A	0.65	Poor	Poor	0.15
B	1.37	Excellent	Poor	0.75
C	0.95	Good	Poor	0.35
D	0.85	Good	Average	1.27

a) Which polymer should Mark choose? Give a reason for your answer.

Polymer ....

Reason ....

....

b) i) It is important for Mark to take the **cost** of the polymer into account. The finished laptop will contain **0.45 kg** of the polymer. If Mark chooses to use polymer B what will be the cost, per laptop, of the polymer?

....

ii) What will be the total spent on the polymer if a batch of **15 000** laptops are made?

....

Section 2.4 — Chemical and Material Behaviour

Metals

Q1 Darius is an **architect**. Each project he works on requires different materials — he chooses the materials for a project based on their **properties**. Use words from the list below to complete the paragraph about the properties of different **metals**.

| copper | aluminium | flexibility | rust | strength | lead |

Some metals like iron have great ...., which makes them ideal for support structures like roof beams. Iron is cheap but will .... if it isn't protected. For some purposes, like window frames, it is important to use a metal that can be easily moulded and is lightweight, e.g. .... All metals conduct electricity, but .... is an exceptionally good conductor so it's often used for electrical wiring.

Q2 Match up the names of the following **metals** to their **properties** and **uses**.

a) **Aluminium**

Corrodes easily unless coated (e.g. with paint)
Hard and tough
High density

Water pipes

b) **Copper**

Lightweight
Resistant to corrosion
Easily moulded

Bicycles

c) **Iron**

Doesn't corrode easily
Ductile
Conducts electricity very well

Gates and railings

Q3 Mae Ling is a **cookware designer**. She is working on a design for a new **pan**. The diagram below shows what the pan could look like when it is finished.

a) What properties of copper make it suitable for the base of the pan?
....
....

— Body of pan
— Pan base — made from copper.

b) The body of the pan needs to be lightweight. Suggest a metal that could be used for this.
....

Section 2.4 — Chemical and Material Behaviour

Metals

Q4 Hector works for a **builders' merchant**. They supply various metals and alloys in different sizes, shapes and lengths. The table shows six of the materials available and some of their **properties**. Use the information in the table to answer the following questions.

Metal	Density (g/cm³)	Melting point (°C)	Malleability	Resistance to corrosion	Strength	Other comments
Steel	7.8	1430	Poor	Poor	Excellent	Very cheap
Solder	9.4	370	Good	Good	Poor	—
Aluminium	2.7	660	Poor	Excellent	Good	—
Lead	11.3	327	Excellent	Good	Poor	Dull, grey colour, toxic
Copper	8.9	1085	Good	Excellent	Average	Excellent conductor
Brass	8.4	940	Good	Good	Average	Shiny, decorative

a) One customer comes into the shop and asks for some **steel** to make a new **window frame**. Give a reason why steel would **not** be a good choice of material to make window frames.

....

b) The builders' merchant used to sell large quantities of **lead**. However, sales of lead have declined over the years.

i) Give one reason why we don't use lead to make fittings such as door handles and taps.

....

ii) Most **water pipes** used to be made from lead. Suggest two reasons why lead was thought to be a good metal for this use.

1. ....

2. ....

iii) Today most water pipes are made from **copper**. Suggest one reason why it is better to make water pipes from copper than lead.

....

c) The builders' merchant supplies **aluminium** to a company that produces small wind turbines that can be attached to a roof to generate electricity. Give two reasons why aluminium is a good choice of material for this use.

1. ....

2. ....

Section 2.4 — Chemical and Material Behaviour

Metal Recycling and Composites

Q1 Tick the correct boxes to show whether the following statements are **true** or **false**.

		True	False
a)	Recycling could help to reduce further increases in greenhouse gas levels.	☐	☐
b)	It is important to recycle metals because there is a finite amount available.	☐	☐
c)	Recycling metals is a cheap and easy process.	☐	☐

Q2 Alan **does not recycle** his cans — he puts them in the rubbish bin.

a) What will happen to the cans he puts in the rubbish?

....

b) Complete the passage using the words in the box.

recycled　　pollute　　metal　　space　　fossil fuels
Landfill sites take up .... and .... the environment. If cans are thrown away rather than being ...., more .... will be used to extract and process .... for new cans.

Q3 Ash is the manager of a rubbish tip. He's thinking of offering **metal recycling** facilities, but before he invests he wants to weigh up the **pros** and **cons**.

Outline two disadvantages of recycling metals.

1. ....

2. ....

Top Tips: Recycling metals is great because it saves resources and reduces the amount of fossil fuels used — the amount of energy saved by recycling one aluminium can is enough to run a TV for three hours. And if that wasn't enough, it also reduces the amount of rubbish sent to landfill.

Section 2.4 — Chemical and Material Behaviour

Metal Recycling and Composites

Q4 Use the words below to complete the paragraph.

strength	combine	bending	steel	durable

Composite materials are mixtures of two other materials — they .... the properties of the materials from which they are made. Reinforced concrete is concrete with metal rods through it (usually made of ....). The concrete gives the composite .... and the rods prevent the structure from .... or stretching. Reinforced concrete is strong and .... and so is widely used in the construction industry.

Q5 The company 'SGT Plastics' produces **glass-reinforced plastic** (GRP). This is a material made of **plastic** reinforced with small fibres of **glass**. Customers can specify the ratio of glass to plastic depending on what they intend to use it for.

a) Give one advantage of using glass-reinforced plastic instead of ordinary plastic.

....

....

....

b) The table shows how the strength of GRP changes with the percentage of glass in the mixture.

Percentage glass	Tensile strength (MPa)
20	132
40	160
60	205
80	245

i) Plot the data on the grid.

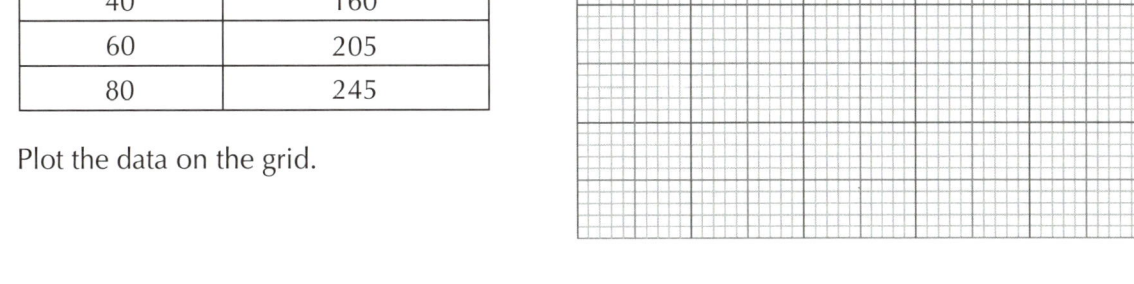

ii) Describe the trend in the graph you have drawn.

....

....

Section 2.4 — Chemical and Material Behaviour

Developing New Materials

Q1 Martin is trying to produce a new material for the **body shell** of **racing cars**. Complete the passage using words from the list below to describe some of the stages that are essential to the development of a new material.

> disposed   availability   damaging   equipment
> recycled   specification   environmental

.... issues must be looked at — the production process must

not be .... and the material must be assessed for how it can

be .... of and ....

.... matching is the stage that makes sure the material does

exactly what it's supposed to do. Price and .... of the

material are also taken into account at this stage. Another important consideration

is safety. During the development of a new material scientists must ensure that both

the material and the .... used to make it are safe.

Q2 Kirsty is developing a new material to be used in **bicycle helmets**.

a) The first stage in the development of a new material is to decide on the **properties** the material will need. She does this by drawing up a specification. Complete the specification using words from the list.

cheap   react   obtainable   heated   lightweight   moulded

- It must be .... and strong.
- It must not .... with water.
- It must be easily .... when ....
- It should be fairly .... and easily ....

b) Kirsty has to make sure the material for the helmet is strong enough to protect the cyclist. Suggest how she can make sure it's safe.

....

....

c) Kirsty must also **design** the **manufacturing process**. Give **two** things that Kirsty needs to consider when designing this process.

1. ....

2. ....

Section 2.4 — Chemical and Material Behaviour

Matching Properties and Uses

Q1 When designing a product, scientists need to be able to **interpret** data about different materials to help them choose one with **suitable properties**. Use the information in the table and graphs below to help answer the questions.

Metal	Thermal conductivity	Electrical conductivity	Strength	Malleability
A	Good	Good	Good	Quite malleable
B	Average	Average	Excellent	Not very malleable
C	Excellent	Excellent	Good	Very malleable
D	Low	Low	Poor	Quite malleable
E	Low	Low	Average	Very malleable

a) What is the density of metal D?

....

b) What is the melting point of metal C?

....

c) Which metal is the best thermal conductor?

....

d) Which metal has a melting point of over 1000 °C but less than 1300 °C?

....

e) List all the metals that have a density outside the range of 6.5 g/cm³ to 10.5 g/cm³.

....

f) For each of the following uses suggest which metal would be most suitable and give a reason for your choice.

   i) support beams ....

   ....

   ii) electrical wire ....

   ....

   iii) saucepan bases ....

   ....

Section 2.4 — Chemical and Material Behaviour

Matching Properties and Uses

Q2 Ken is building a **garage** on the side of his house.
He has drawn up the following **design specification**.

- Strong and sturdy walls.
- Solid foundations.
- Waterproof and secure roof.
- Windows for workshop area at the rear.
- Secure entrance.

a) The garage needs to have a **roof**.

   i) Suggest a reason why **iron** would not be a suitable material for the roof.

   ....

   ii) Suggest a material that could be used for the roof and give a reason for your choice.

   ....

b) Give one advantage of using **ceramic bricks** to build the walls of the garage.

   ....

c) To ensure the garage is secure Ken decided to use **glass-reinforced plastic** for the windows. What is the advantage of using a composite instead of ordinary glass?

   ....

d) i) Which of the following would be the most suitable material for the **door handles**?
      Tick the correct box.

      Iron   ☐
      Wood   ☐
      Plastic   ☐

   ii) Explain why you chose this material.

   ....

e) Ken used **concrete** for the foundations. Give two reasons why concrete is well suited to this use.

   1. ....
   2. ....

Top Tips: As you may well have guessed, this section was all about being able to select the right materials for a job. If you're asked to pick a suitable material in the exam, don't panic — just think carefully about the properties you need. There'll be one out there that suits the job perfectly.

Section 2.4 — Chemical and Material Behaviour

Mixed Questions for Sections 2.3 and 2.4

Q1 Gemma is **cleaning** the **kitchen** after having some friends over for dinner.

    a) She cleans the **ceramic** tiles with soap and water.

        i) Give **two** characteristic properties of ceramics.

            1. ....

            2. ....

        ii) What is the chemical formula for water? ....

    b) Gemma is clearing away some of the drinks she made for her friends. For each of the following mixtures, **circle** the **solvent** and **underline** the **solute(s)**.

        i) A cup of tea made with boiling water and one sugar.

        ii) A soluble indigestion tablet in a glass of water.

        iii) Carbon dioxide in fizzy water.

    c) Gemma then cleans the oven with a **foam oven cleaner**. Describe the composition of a foam.

    ....

    ....

    d) One of the ingredients in Gemma's oven cleaner is **ammonia**.

        i) What is the chemical formula for ammonia? ....

        ii) Ammonia is a **bulk chemical**. What does this mean?

            ....

        iii) Is ammonia an organic or inorganic chemical? ....

Q2 Hazleen works for a company that makes **fireworks**. One of the chemicals used in firework production is **barium chloride**.

    a) Barium chloride reacts with sodium sulfate in the following reaction:

        barium chloride + sodium sulfate → barium sulfate + sodium chloride

    Write a symbol equation for the reaction. It has been balanced for you.

        .... + ... → .... + 2....................

    b) One of the products, sodium chloride, is an **ionic** compound.
Give three characteristic properties of ionic compounds.

        1. ....

        2. ....

        3. ....

Mixed Questions for Sections 2.3 and 2.4

Q3 Jack is designing a new house for himself.

a) He chooses to use **reinforced concrete** as one of the building materials. Give one way in which reinforced concrete is better than normal concrete.

....

....

b) Jack buys a new **kettle** for his house. The kettle is **metal** with a **plastic** handle.

   i) What properties will the polymer used to make the handle have?
   Circle the correct answer(s).

       low melting point   good thermal insulator   good thermal conductor   high melting point

   ii) What is the plastic used to make the handle likely to be derived from?

   ....

   iii) The metal is **recycled**. Give one advantage and one disadvantage of recycling metals.

   Advantage ....

   ....

   Disadvantage ....

   ....

c) The **electrical wiring** in Jack's house will be made of **copper**.
Give three reasons why copper is a good choice for this use.

   1. ....

   2. ....

   3. ....

d) Each of the following materials will be used in the house. Write the chemical symbol for each.

   i) Calcium carbonate ....   ii) Lead ....

   iii) Silicon ....   iv) Aluminium ....

e) Jack decides that he wants the interior walls of his house to be painted blue. The **paint** he chooses is an **emulsion**. Describe the composition of an emulsion.

....

....

Section 2.5 — Energy, Electricity and Radiation

Fossil Fuels

Q1 Most of the UK's **electricity** is generated using **non-renewable** energy sources.

a) Explain the difference between 'renewable' and 'non-renewable' energy sources.

....

....

b) From those given below, **circle** the renewable energy sources and **underline** the non-renewable energy sources.

coal   waves   natural gas   hydroelectric   wind   oil

tidal   solar   biomass   nuclear   geothermal

Q2 Fill in the blanks in the paragraph below using words from the box.

| renewable | natural gas | burning | fossil |
| oxygen | remains | energy | non-renewable |

Coal, oil and .... are all .... fuels.

They are .... and are formed over millions of years

from the .... of dead animals and plants. They are a

source of .... — this is released from the fuels by

.... them in ....

Q3 Joe is an environmental campaigner. He has spent the day in the city, handing out leaflets to help inform people about the **environmental problems** caused by products made from **crude oil**.

a) Give **three** consumer products that are made from crude oil.

....

b) Crude oil is a **fossil fuel**. Match each environmental problem associated with fossil fuels to its cause. Some problems may have the same cause.

Acid rain

Rising CO$_2$ levels in the atmosphere

Climate change

Pollution of rivers

Releasing CO$_2$ by burning fossil fuels

Sulfur dioxide formed by burning oil and coal

Coal mining

Fossil Fuels

Q4 James is an environmental scientist working for an energy company. He has been investigating **alternative fuels** to use.

Fuel	Cost (pence per kg)	Heat Content (kJ per kg)
Coal	11	34 000
Wood	5	20 000
Ethanol	130	30 000
Methane (natural gas)	60	56 000

a) Which of the fuels in the table will release the **most energy** when burnt?

   ....

b) Which of the fuels in the table is the most **expensive**?

   ....

c) Give a reason why the fuels in the table are **easy** to use.

   ....

d) Suggest which of the fuels would be the easiest to **store**. ....

e) i) Which **two** fuels in the table are non-renewable fossil fuels?

   ....

   ii) Give one **non-environmental** problem associated with the use of non-renewable fuels.

   ....

   ....

f) Give one **advantage** of using fossil fuels, in terms of availability in the **short-term**.

   ....

g) What do you think will have happened to the cost of coal in fifty years time? Explain your answer.

   ....

   ....

Top Tips: Fossil fuels — it's a sad story. Not only are they harming the environment, but they're going to run out very soon. The world is going to have no choice but to look at alternative fuels to keep their MP3 players charged, as you'll find out on the next pages.

Section 2.5 — Energy, Electricity and Radiation

Alternative Energy Resources

Q1 Write the five **fuels** given below in the correct columns of the table to indicate their **fuel type**.

uranium   wood   coal   oil   natural gas

Fossil	Nuclear	Biomass

Q2 About 20% of the UK's electricity comes from **nuclear power stations** — the majority is still produced by burning **fossil fuels**.

   a) Write down one advantage and one disadvantage of nuclear power compared to using fossil fuels to generate electricity.

   Advantage ....

   ....

   Disadvantage ....

   ....

   b) Describe how building a nuclear power plant can have a positive impact on its surrounding area.

   ....

Q3 Chloe works in a **nuclear power plant** — she's explaining to a group of visitors how it's powered. Complete the passage below using the words in the box.

nuclear fuel	radioactive	energy

Some elements (for example, uranium) are .... and give out .... in the form of radiation. These elements can be used as .... in nuclear power stations.

Top Tips: Nuclear fuel can provide **millions** of times more energy than the same mass of fossil fuel. With the current concerns about CO_2 emissions from burning fossil fuels, you can see why people see nuclear fuel as an attractive alternative. It's important not to forget about the nuclear waste though.

Section 2.5 — Energy, Electricity and Radiation

Alternative Energy Resources

Q4 The map below shows a small island. Five sites are labelled A - E. These are the proposed sites of different **energy developments**. Environmental scientists are assessing the potential of each site.

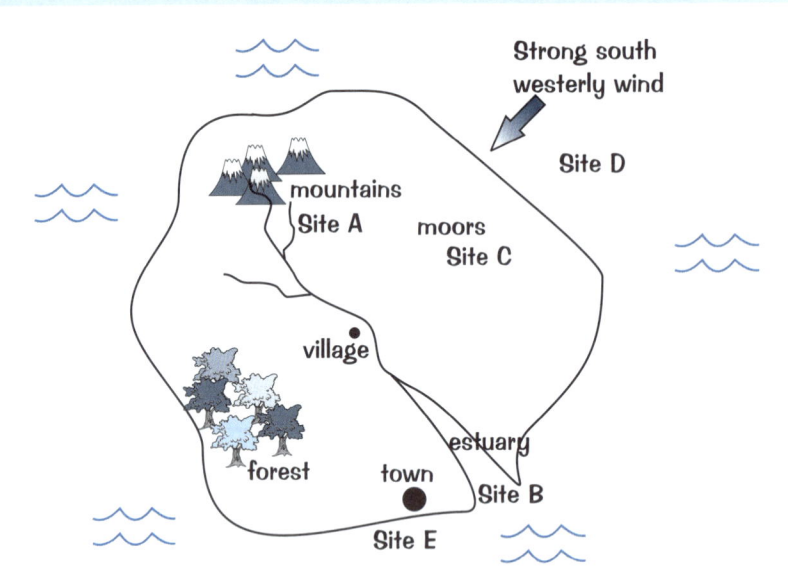

a) i) Which two sites would be most suitable for a **wind farm**? Explain why.

....
....

ii) What are the advantages of wind turbines?
Tick **two** boxes from the list below.

☐ They are quiet.   ☐ They cause virtually no pollution.

☐ They produce electricity constantly.   ☐ Their fuel is free.

b) i) Which site would be most suitable for a **hydroelectric power station**? Explain why.

....
....

ii) Give one advantage and one disadvantage of using hydroelectric power.

....
....

c) i) Which site would be most suitable for a **tidal barrage**? Explain why.

....

ii) Give one advantage and one disadvantage of using tidal barrages to produce electricity.

....
....

Section 2.5 — Energy, Electricity and Radiation

Alternative Energy Resources

Q5 Mary is considering having **solar panels** installed on her roof to produce her electricity.

Explain the advantages and disadvantages of using solar cells to generate electricity.

....

....

....

Q6 'Pelamis' is a 450-foot long **wave-powered generator** prototype off the coast of the Orkney Islands in Scotland.

a) What are the advantages of wave power? Circle the two correct answers.

no pollution   **very reliable**   **low set up costs**   **no fuel costs**

b) What are the disadvantages of wave power? Circle the two correct answers.

high pollution   **high set-up costs**   **unreliable**   **high running costs**

Q7 Mr Saleem is a cattle farmer in India. He has just installed a small **biogas** plant on his farm.

a) What is meant by 'biogas'?

....

b) What source of biogas is Mr Saleem likely to use?

....

c) Apart from cooking and heating, how else could Mr Saleem make use of the biogas?

....

d) Give two **advantages** of using biofuels rather than fossil fuels.

1. ....

2. ....

Top Tips: Burning animal poo is nothing new — people have been doing it for years, and many still do. For instance, if you're a nomadic yak herder in Mongolia, you probably don't have **mains electricity**, but you **do** have lots of **yak poo**. Dry it, burn it, and you'll have a nice warm tent.

Section 2.5 — Energy, Electricity and Radiation

Energy Transfer

Q1 There are many different forms of **energy**.

   a) Use some of the words below to fill in the gaps in the paragraph.

> created   destroyed   use   stay the same
> preservation   converted   space   form

The principle of conservation of energy says that energy can't be

.... or .... The total amount of energy

in the Universe will always .... — it just gets

.... from one .... to another.

   b) Write down five different forms of energy.

1. ....
2. ....
3. ....
4. ....
5. ....

Andy got 4 out of 5. Close, but no cigar.

Q2 Rob has just moved into a new house, and decides to buy a new **stereo** to go in the lounge. His new stereo can play tapes and CDs, and has backlit buttons.

For each of the following scenarios, fill in the gaps to describe the **energy transfers** taking place.

   a) A light comes on when a button is pressed.

.... energy ➡ .... energy

   b) The stereo reads a CDs digital audio signal using a laser.

.... energy ➡ .... energy

   c) A noise comes from the vibrating cone in the speaker.

.... energy ➡ .... energy

   d) The stereo is left switched on for a long time, and its back becomes warm.

.... energy ➡ .... energy

Section 2.5 — Energy, Electricity and Radiation

Generating Electricity

Q1 The diagram below shows a **power station**.

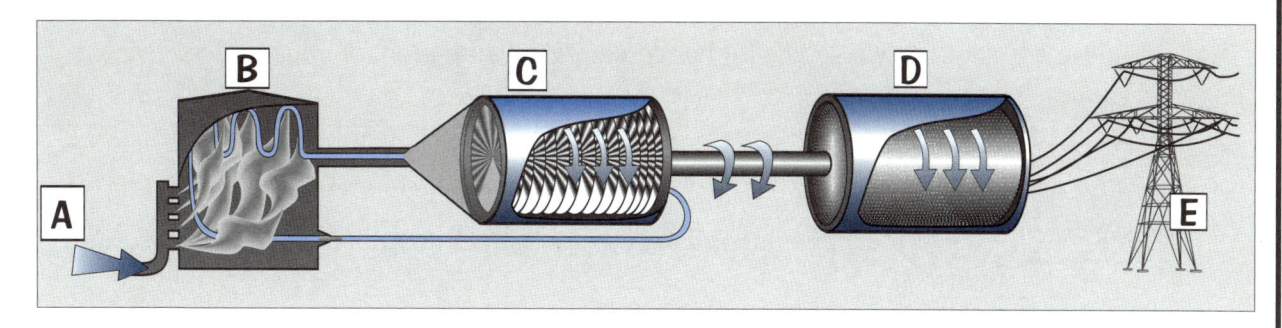

a) Draw lines to match up the parts of the diagram with the appropriate sentences.

- A — The steam produced is used to turn a turbine.
- B — The electricity is delivered via a network of cables.
- C — The fuel is burnt and the heat energy is used to boil water.
- D — Fuel (e.g. coal, oil, or gas) enters the boiler.
- E — The turbine rotates a generator to create electricity.

b) Energy is **converted** into different forms (including kinetic, electrical, heat and chemical energy) within a power station.

i) Which type of energy is contained in the **fuel**? ....

ii) Which type of energy is produced in part **B**? ....

iii) Which type of energy is produced in part **C**? ....

iv) Which type of energy does the power station **produce**? ....

c) Why isn't the process of producing energy in power stations very efficient?

....

d) i) What is the **National Grid**?

....

....

ii) Explain why electricity is a useful way of supplying energy to homes.

....

....

Section 2.5 — Energy, Electricity and Radiation

Energy in the Home

Q1 Helen has bought a new **house** near the centre of **town**. Choose a suitable **power source** for each of her appliances and give a reason for your choice.

a) Choose a suitable power source for her **cooker**, giving a reason for your choice.

   i) Power source ....

   ii) Reason for choice ....

   ....

b) Choose a suitable power source for her **television**, giving a reason for your choice.

   i) Power source ....

   ii) Reason for choice ....

   ....

c) Helen's previous home was a farmhouse in an **isolated** area of **countryside**. What was the likely **power source** for her **central heating**? Give a reason for your choice.

   i) Power source ....

   ii) Reason for choice ....

   ....

Q2 Richard lives in the countryside and has just received a delivery of **solid fuel** from his supplier.

a) Circle the correct word in each pair to complete the following passage on solid fuels.

   Solid fuels like wood and oil / coal are a relatively cheap / expensive source of energy.

   They're usually used for transport / heating and are harder / easier to store than natural gas.

b) Richard goes out later to get some fuel for his car. Give two fuels suitable for use in vehicles.

   ....

Q3 Fred usually powers his **laptop computer** by plugging it into the mains electricity. He is considering buying a **battery** to power it instead.

Give one **advantage** and one **disadvantage** of using a battery to power a laptop.

Advantage: ....

Disadvantage: ....

Top Tips: Make sure you know your batteries from your plug sockets and your oil from your gas. It's useful to be able to weigh up which power sources would be most useful for different things.

Section 2.5 — Energy, Electricity and Radiation

Using Energy Efficiently

Q1 Kaitlin is shopping for a new **fridge** and is keen to buy an **efficient** one. The shop assistant at Fridge Universe tells her, wrongly, that the more efficient the fridge, the **colder** it keeps your food.

Fill in the gaps in the following passage using words from the box to explain what is really meant by the efficiency of an appliance. You can use words more than once.

| efficient | sound | hot | most | input | wasted | noise |
| electrical | used | heat | surroundings | useful | little |

Electrical appliances have an .... of ....
energy. Not all of this is converted into .... energy. Some of
the energy is .... This energy does not disappear — it is still
there but in forms which can't be easily .... Energy is often
wasted as .... or .... energy. Efficient
appliances transfer .... of the energy from one form to another
with .... energy loss to the ....
Inefficient appliances transfer .... of the energy from one form
to another with .... energy being lost to the
....

Heaters are an exception to this — they're designed to give out a lot of energy to the surroundings.

Q2 Tick the boxes to show whether these statements are **true** or **false**. **True False**

a) The total energy supplied to a machine is called the **total energy input**. ☐ ☐

b) The **useful energy output** of a machine is never more than its total energy input. ☐ ☐

c) The **wasted energy** from a machine is the energy it delivers that's not useful. ☐ ☐

d) The more **efficient** a machine is, the more energy it **wastes**. ☐ ☐

Q3 Here is the **energy flow diagram** for an **electric lamp**. Complete the sentences below.

energy input 100 J → light energy output 5 J
↓ heat energy output

a) The total **energy input** is .... J

b) The **useful energy output** is .... J

c) The amount of energy **wasted** is .... J

Section 2.5 — Energy, Electricity and Radiation

Using Energy Efficiently

Q4 John was concerned that he was **using too much energy** in his home.

Explain why it would be beneficial to John to reduce the amount of energy he uses.

....

Q5 Sophie wants to know what type of **energy** her appliances **waste** energy as.

Draw lines to connect the **output** energy arrows with the correct **energy** type(s).

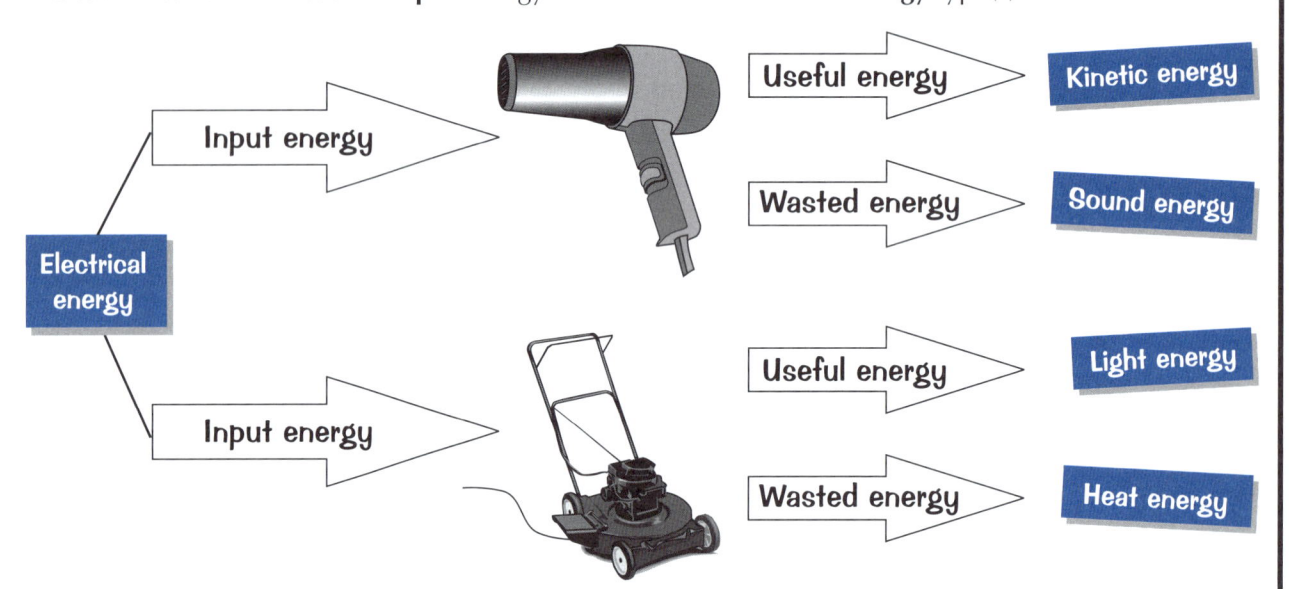

Q6 Mark is looking for a new **lawn mower** — his local garden centre has three. He wants to know which one is the most **efficient**. The table shows how much energy is converted into **useful** energy and how much is **wasted** by each lawn mower.

Lawn mower	Input energy (J)	Useful output energy (J)	Wasted output energy (J)	Efficiency (%)
1	200	160		
2	550		130	
3		900	345	

a) Fill in the missing energy figures in the table.

b) Calculate the efficiency of each device, using the formula:

$$\text{Efficiency} = \frac{\text{Useful output energy}}{\text{Input energy}} \times 100\%$$

Top Tips: Efficiency is one of those rare topics in physics that makes sense — if you put loads of energy into a machine, but get little useful energy out in return, your machine isn't efficient. Easy.

Section 2.5 — Energy, Electricity and Radiation

Using Energy Efficiently

Q7 For a school project, Ashley is given the **input** and **output** energies for certain household appliances and must calculate the **efficiency** of each device. For each of the appliances below, circle the **useful** energy output(s), and calculate the **efficiency** of each device.

a) 250 J Input energy → Hair straighteners → 240 J heat energy output in the heating plates
→ 10 J heat energy output in the handles

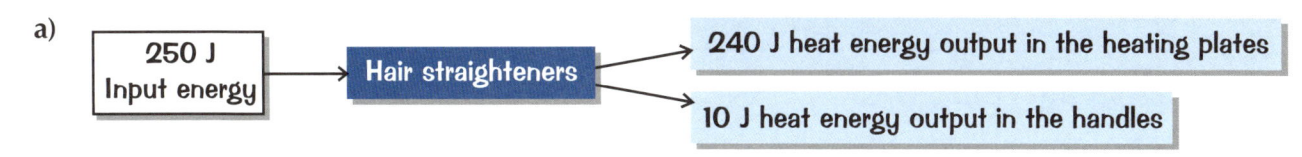

Efficiency = ...

b) 550 J Input energy → Filament lamp → 44 J output light energy
→ 506 J output heat energy

Efficiency = ...

c) 700 J Input energy → Washing machine → 150 J kinetic energy output turning the drum
→ 150 J output sound energy
→ 300 J heat energy output in the water
→ 100 J heat energy output in the body of the machine

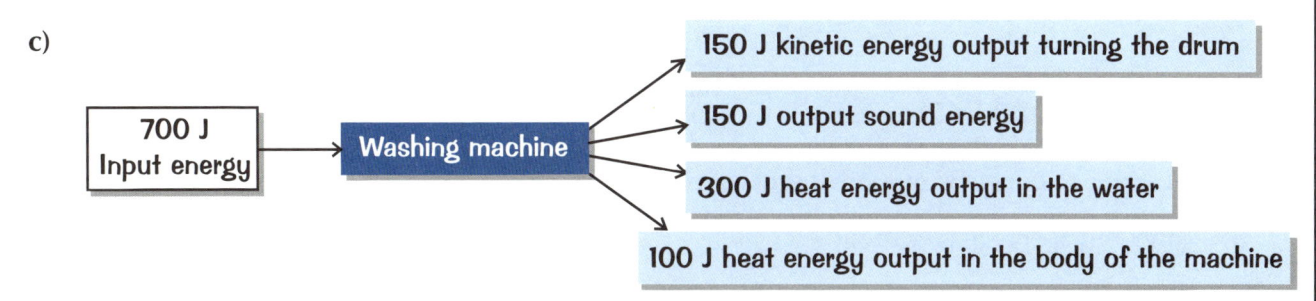

Efficiency = ...

Q8 Clive is researching different kinds of **electric light bulb**. He finds the following information.

	Low-energy bulb	Ordinary bulb
Electrical energy input per second (J)	15	60
Light energy output per second (J)	1.4	1.4
Cost	£3.50	50p
Typical expected lifetime	8 years	1 year
Estimated annual running cost	£1.00	£4.00

a) Which type of bulb is more efficient? Explain your answer.

....

b) Write down an **advantage** to **Clive** of using a **low-energy** light bulb.

....

c) Write down an **advantage** to **society** of more people using low energy bulbs.

....

Section 2.5 — Energy, Electricity and Radiation

Sankey Diagrams

Q1 This diagram shows the energy changes in a **toy crane**. The diagram is drawn to scale.

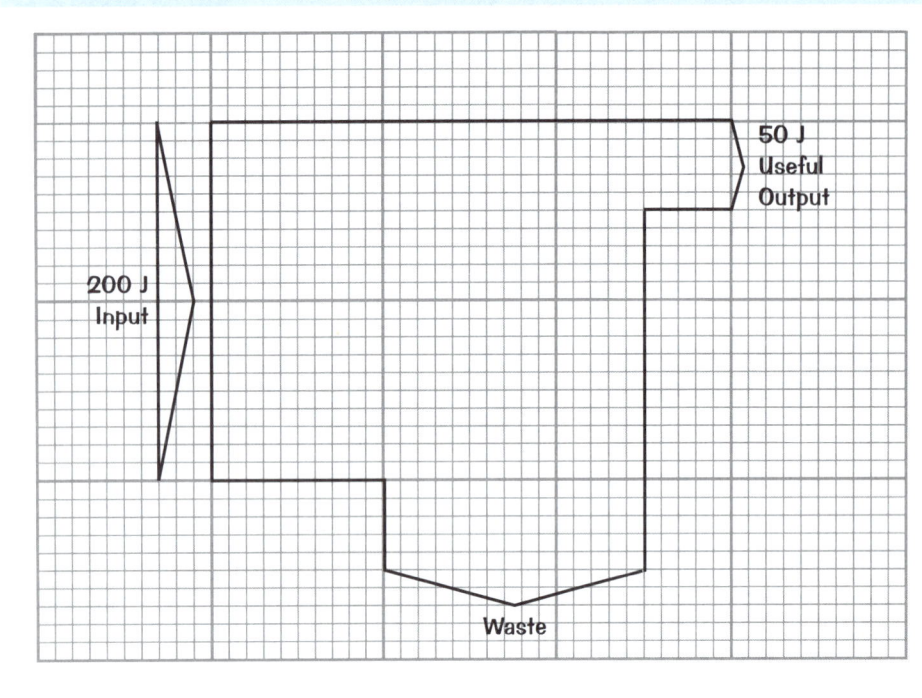

[Diagram: 200 J Input → 50 J Useful Output, with Waste branch]

a) How much energy is **one small square** worth? .... J

b) How much energy is **wasted**? .... J

Q2 The Sankey diagram below is for a **winch** — a machine which **lifts** objects on hooks and cables.

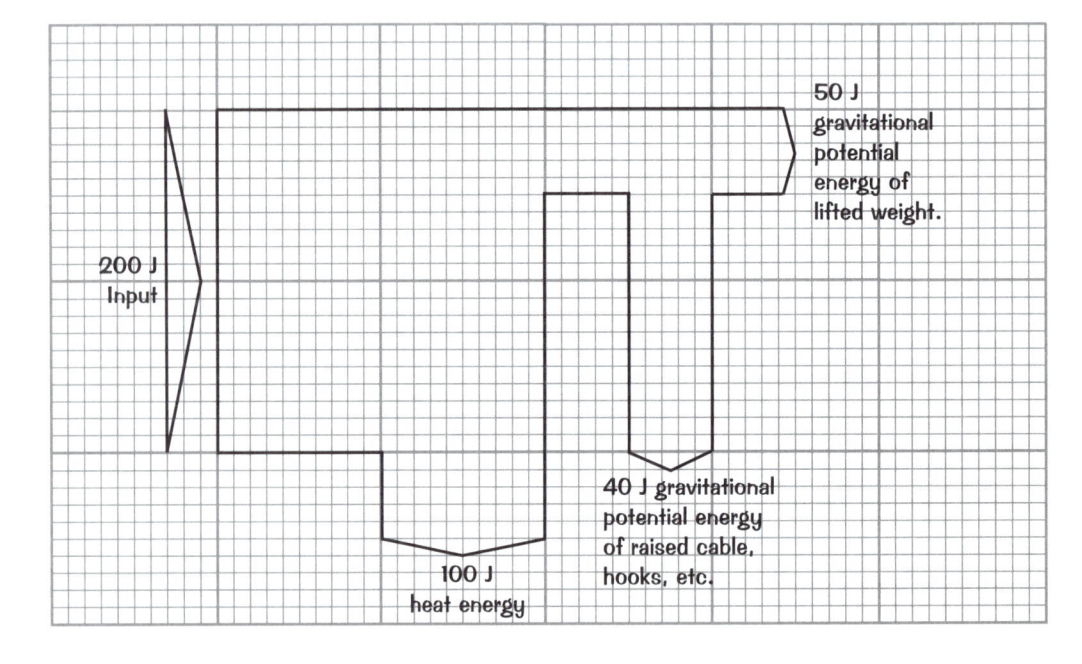

[Diagram: 200 J Input → 50 J gravitational potential energy of lifted weight; 40 J gravitational potential energy of raised cable, hooks, etc.; 100 J heat energy]

a) What is the total amount of energy **wasted**? .... J

b) How much useful **gravitational energy** is produced? .... J

Section 2.5 — Energy, Electricity and Radiation

Calculating Power and Current

Q1 Janet wants to calculate the **power** of some of her appliances.
Circle the correct **formula** below for calculating power in a circuit.

$$\text{power} = \frac{\text{voltage}}{\text{current}}$$

$$\text{power} = \text{voltage} \times \text{current}$$

$$\text{power} = \frac{\text{current}}{\text{voltage}}$$

Q2 Martin wants to know what the **electrical information** on the sticker on the back of his computer means.

Draw lines to match the electrical quantities to their correct symbols and units.

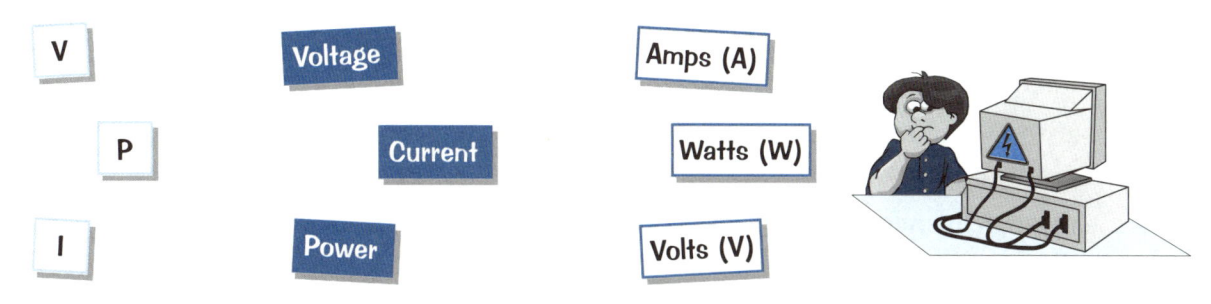

V		Voltage		Amps (A)
P		Current		Watts (W)
I		Power		Volts (V)

Q3 Robert has a number of **electrical components** and is not sure of their **power ratings**. He tests each of the components, using an appropriate power supply for each one. He designs a table to record the results.

You need to learn the formula for power.

Complete the table by calculating the power of each component.

Component	Voltage	Current	Power
Microphone	12	10	
Lamp	12		24
Buzzer	230		1380
Motor	230	3.2	

Section 2.5 — Energy, Electricity and Radiation

Calculating Energy Usage and Cost

Q1 Clara is trying to reduce the amount of **electricity** she uses. Below are some of the **household appliances** she uses most often and their **power ratings**.

Number the appliances in order of how much they would **cost** if they were all left on for the **same amount of time**. Make number one the most expensive, and number six the cheapest.

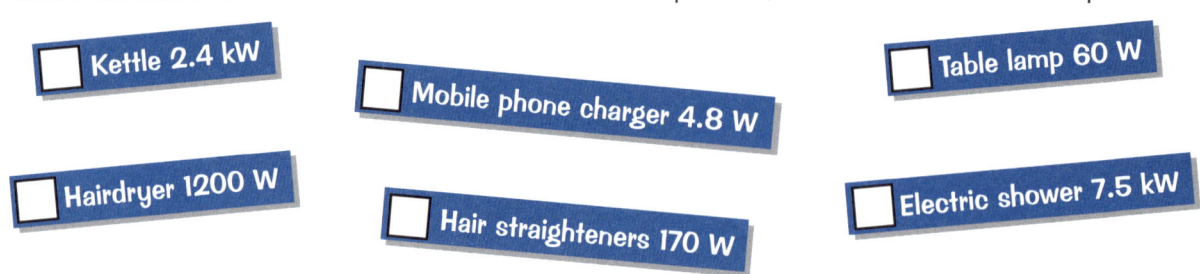

- ☐ Kettle 2.4 kW
- ☐ Mobile phone charger 4.8 W
- ☐ Table lamp 60 W
- ☐ Hairdryer 1200 W
- ☐ Hair straighteners 170 W
- ☐ Electric shower 7.5 kW

Q2 Using the formula **power = energy ÷ time**, calculate the **power** of the following **appliances**.

Don't forget energy is in joules and time is in seconds.

a) A **radio** that converts 40 J of energy into heat and sound energy in 2 seconds.

....

b) An **electric blender** that converts 18 kJ of energy into kinetic, heat and sound energy in 1 minute.

....

c) A **toaster** that converts 153 kJ of energy into heat energy in 90 seconds.

....

Q3 Richard thinks that he is using too much **electricity** in his home and that his electricity bill will be very **expensive**. He draws a table to help him work out if he is right.

Appliance	Power (kW)	Time left on (hours)	Energy used (kWh)	Cost (p)
Electric heater	2	3	6	120
Travel iron	1.2	0.5		
Surround sound hi-fi	0.5	1.5		
Light bulb	0.06	3.25		

a) Calculate the electrical energy used by each appliance. The first one has been done for you.

b) The Wattless Electricity Company charges **20p per kWh**. Complete the table by calculating how much each appliance costs to run for the time given. Round your answers to the nearest penny. The first one has been done for you.

Section 2.5 — Energy, Electricity and Radiation

Calculating Energy Usage and Cost

Q4 The last time Anthony read his **electricity meter**, it read **6582 kWh**. The diagram below shows what his meter reads now.

| 0 | 0 | 0 | 9 | 8 | 1 | 4 | 5 |

The last number shows tenths of a kWh.

a) How much electricity has Anthony used since he last checked his meter?

....

b) Anthony's electricity supplier charges **11p per kWh**. Calculate how much Anthony has spent on electricity since he last read his meter.

....

Q5 Mr Havel recently received his **electricity bill**. Unfortunately, he tore off the bottom part to write a shopping list.

Customer : Havel, V

Date: Meter Reading:

11 / 06 / 06   34259 kWh
10 / 09 / 06   34783 kWh

Total Cost @ 9.7p per kWh

a) How many **kWh** of energy did Mr Havel use in the three months from June to September?

....

b) Calculate Mr Havel's bill for the three months to the nearest penny.

....

....

Q6 Tina's mum grumbles at her for leaving a 0.06 kW lamp on overnight — about 9 hours every night. Tina says her mum uses **more energy** by using an 8 kW shower for 0.25 hours every day.

Is Tina right? Calculate how much energy each person uses and compare your results.

....

....

....

....

Top Tips: Although there's quite a bit of maths on these pages, it's nothing too difficult. There's two formulae you need to be able to use — one to work out power and one to calculate cost.

Section 2.5 — Energy, Electricity and Radiation

Heat Transfer

Q1 Max wants to know which type of **heat transfer** occurs in which situations. Complete the table by putting a tick in the correct column(s) to match each property to the type of heat transfer. A property can apply to more than one type of heat transfer.

		Thermal radiation	Conduction	Convection
a)	Only occurs in liquids and gases			
b)	How we feel heat from the Sun			
c)	Occurs in solids, liquids and gases			
d)	Vibrating particles pass their energy to their neighbours			
e)	Higher energy particles in the hotter region move to the cooler region			
f)	Occurs mainly in solids			

Q2 **Heat transfer** to or from an **object** depends on its temperature and the **temperature** of its **surroundings**.

a) Calculate the temperature difference between the following objects and their surroundings.

A Hot kettle: temperature is 100 °C, temperature of surroundings is 21 °C ....

B Soldering iron tip: temperature is 280 °C, temperature of surroundings is 22 °C ....

C Snowman: temperature is −1 °C, temperature of surroundings is 4 °C ....

b) Put the objects, A-C, in part a) in order according to how quickly heat is transferred to or from the surroundings. Start with the slowest.

The bigger the temperature difference, the faster heat is transferred to the surroundings.

..................................,.................................,.................................

Q3 Simon is doing a project on **heat transfer in the home**. Help him out by explaining how heat is transferred in each of the following situations.

a) How heat is transferred from the electric ring on the hob to milk in a pan on top of it.

....

....

b) How heat is transferred from the Sun to the air inside a greenhouse.

....

....

Section 2.5 — Energy, Electricity and Radiation

Heat Transfer

Q4 **Convection** can make **water flow** round the **pipes** in a house, without using a pump. Miss Jenkins demonstrates this to her pupils using the apparatus below.

a) Draw arrows on the diagram to show which way the water moves.

b) Number the boxes to explain what happens to the water above the heat to cause the convection current.

- [ ] The water expands as its temperature increases.
- [ ] The temperature of the water increases.
- [ ] The warm water floats upwards and is replaced by denser cold water from the right.
- [ ] The water is heated by conduction.
- [ ] The water becomes less dense as it expands.

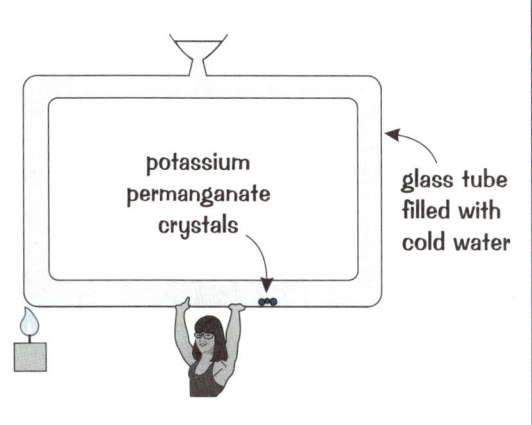

Q5 An energy efficiency consultant is using a **thermal imaging camera** to perform a heat loss survey on a house. It works by detecting the **infrared radiation** emitted by different parts of the building— the hotter the area, the brighter it will appear.

Use the diagram below to fill in the blanks to complete the consultant's explanation of what he sees.

The thermal imaging camera shows that the windows are .... than their surroundings. This means they emit .... radiation than they absorb. This makes the house .... down.

The external walls of the house are dark, which means they are .... than their surroundings. They emit .... radiation than they absorb, so they cause the house to gradually .... up.

Top Tips: Clever people don't wear thick jumpers when it's cold out. Oh no. They put on two thinnish jumpers — to **trap air** between the layers and reduce their heat losses by convection and conduction. Then, they wrap themselves in tinfoil — to reduce their heat losses by radiation.

Section 2.5 — Energy, Electricity and Radiation

Heat Transfer in the Home

Q1 Don is thinking about fitting **loft insulation** to reduce his heating bill.

Circle the correct word in the sentence to explain what insulation is.

Insulation helps reduce unwanted energy / efficiency transfers.

Q2 Mrs Diggles is interested in improving the energy **efficiency** of the flat where she lives.

a) Calculate the payback time for the improvements shown in the table.

Improvement	Initial cost	Annual saving	Payback time (years)
Double glazing	£1500	£50	
Hot-water tank jacket	£10	£15	
Draught proofing	£40	£40	
Loft insulation	£210	£70	

b) Explain the two ways double glazing reduces heat loss.

....

....

c) Mrs Diggles plans to move out of the flat in 10 months time. Which improvement would you recommend? Give a reason for your answer.

....

....

Q3 Enid the **energy consultant** is on her way to work in the snow. She spots this house on the way.

Enid thinks the house could do with an energy survey.

a) Why does she think the house could be losing a lot of heat?

....

....

b) Suggest **one** step the owner could take to reduce the heat loss.

....

Section 2.5 — Energy, Electricity and Radiation

Heat Transfer in the Home

Q4 Jake is having a **new house** built. The designer is explaining ways that he can **reduce heat loss**. Draw lines to match the following ways to reduce heat loss from the home with their correct descriptions.

Hot water tank jacket	Each window has two layers of glass instead of one
Draught proofing	Foam is installed in the gap between the inner and outer layer of bricks
Central heating room thermostat	A thick layer of fibreglass is laid out across the whole loft floor
Loft insulation	A thick insulating material is wrapped around the hot water tank
Double glazing	Gaps around doors, windows and floors are plugged with foam, plastic or paper
Cavity wall insulation	Switches the heating off when the inside of the house reaches a set temperature and back on when the temperature drops

Q5 To try and encourage people to insulate their homes, the Government have made grants available to some people to help pay for **insulation**. Energy Planet World has produced an information leaflet giving typical **prices** and estimated **savings** for various types of houses.

Type of house	Full price of insulation	Grant (if eligible)	Estimated saving per year
2 bed end terrace	£300	£50	£50
3 bed semi-detached	£375	£75	£60
4 bed semi-detached	£455	£125	£80

a) Mary wants to reduce her heating bills. She lives in a three-bed semi detached house and is eligible for a grant. What is the payback time if she installs cavity wall insulation?

....

b) Describe how cavity wall insulation reduces the amount of heat lost from a house.

....

....

Section 2.5 — Energy, Electricity and Radiation

Heat Exchangers

Q1 Use the words in the box to complete the passage below.

easy	heat exchangers	spread out	difficult	heat

Energy is usually wasted as .... energy. Wasted energy tends to ...., which makes it .... to capture and re-use. .... enable waste energy to be captured and recycled.

Q2 Michael is an engineer working on the **heating system** of a new **car**.

a) The diagram to the right shows the **heater core** he has designed. The heater core is a heat exchanger that is used to heat the inside of the car. Label the arrows with either 'hot coolant' or 'cold coolant'.

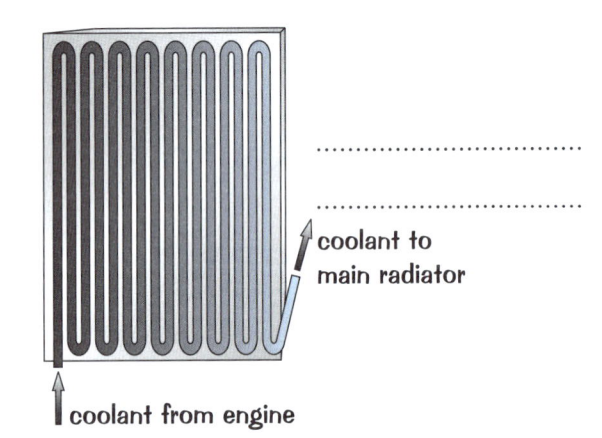

coolant to main radiator

coolant from engine

b) The following sentences describe how the heater system works. Number the boxes to put the sequence in the correct order. The first one has been done for you.

[ ] Heat is emitted from the coolant into the heater core.

[ ] Heat is emitted from the heater core into the inside of the car.

[1] Cold coolant absorbs heat from the engine.

[ ] Hot coolant moves from the engine to the heater core.

Michael loved to heat a core or two.

Q3 Ann is a **refrigerator** salesperson. She is often asked to explain how fridges **keep cool**. Ann explains that the fridge has a heat exchanger. Complete the following explanation using words in the list.

back	reflected	surroundings	front	absorbed	food

Heat inside a fridge is .... by coolant in the fridge's cooling system. Warm coolant travels to the .... of the fridge where it is transferred to the .... by a heat exchanger.

Section 2.5 — Energy, Electricity and Radiation

Electromagnetic Waves

Q1 **Communication engineers** need to know about **electromagnetic waves** to carry out their job properly. Draw lines to complete the three sentences about electromagnetic waves.

Electromagnetic radiation — the distance from one peak to the next.

Wavelength is — the number of waves produced by a source per second.

Frequency is — travels as waves.

Q2 **Electromagnetic radiation** occurs at many different **wavelengths**.

a) Complete the table to show the seven types of EM waves:

			VISIBLE LIGHT			
1m–10^4m	10^{-2}m (3cm)	10^{-5}m (0.01mm)	10^{-7}m	10^{-8}m	10^{-10}m	10^{-12}m

b) Circle the correct word in each pair to complete the following sentence.

The left hand regions of the EM spectrum shown above have **higher** / **lower** frequencies and **longer** / **shorter** wavelengths than the right hand regions.

Q3 Diagrams **A**, **B** and **C** represent electromagnetic waves.

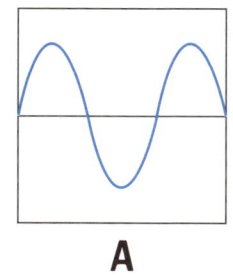

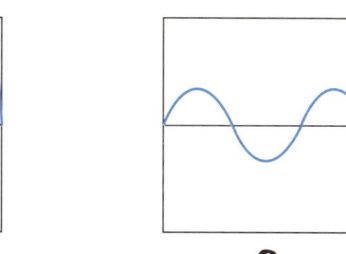

A   **B**   **C**

a) Which two diagrams show waves with the same **frequency**? .... and ....

b) Which two diagrams show waves with the same **wavelength**? .... and ....

Top Tips:
The important thing on this page is to know what the definitions of wavelength and frequency are (as well as knowing the different types of electromagnetic waves, of course).

Section 2.5 — Energy, Electricity and Radiation

Uses of Electromagnetic Waves

Q1 Radio waves with extremely long wavelengths are used to communicate between submarines and inside mines.

Give two more common uses of radio waves.

1. ....

2. ....

Q2 Molly makes a call on her mobile phone to Tara's mobile phone, some distance away. Complete the passage to describe how the signal travels from Molly's to Tara's phone.

| X-rays | mast | pipes | microwaves | cables | satellite | nearest |

The .... emitted by Molly's mobile phone are picked up by the nearest mobile phone .... This transmits the signal through the central mobile telephone exchange, where it passes to the mast .... Tara's phone. That mast then emits the signal as microwaves, which are detected by Tara's phone.

Q3 Froggarts County police are using thermal imaging to track a burglar.

Use the words in the box below to complete the passage about thermal imaging.

| cool | temperature | warmer | infrared |
| warm | cooler |

Thermal imagers sense .... energy and create a .... pattern. .... objects stand out from the .... background.

Top Tips: Radio waves with different wavelengths are used and transmitted in different ways. Some waves bend around the Earth's surface, some are reflected off a layer of the atmosphere, and others are sent directly to a receiver. All you need to do now is transmit this stuff to your brain.

Section 2.5 — Energy, Electricity and Radiation

Uses of Electromagnetic Waves

Q4 Julia is experimenting with the **remote control** units for her family's TV set and DVD player. Remote control units work by sending a beam of **infrared waves** to a receptor on the television or other device.

a) Number the following types of electromagnetic waves in order of wavelength, from shortest to longest wavelength.

☐ visible light   ☐ ultraviolet waves   ☐ infrared waves

b) How can you tell that the remotes do **not** use visible light?

....

c) Use statements A-D to answer the following questions.

> A — Infrared waves can be transmitted through glass.
> B — Infrared waves can be reflected off walls or furniture.
> C — Infrared waves cannot pass through any solid object.
> D — Infrared waves cannot pass through opaque solid objects.

Opaque means the opposite of transparent. An opaque object is something you can't see through.

i) Julia changes TV channels using the remote control unit. She notices that even if she is holding it backwards it still works. What does this tell her about infrared waves? ....

ii) Julia's DVD machine is in a cabinet with a glass door. She finds she can use the DVD remote even when this door is closed. What does this tell her about infrared waves? ....

iii) Julia notices that if a magazine is placed in front of the receptor on the base of the TV then the TV remote cannot be used. The same happens if furniture or people block the path of the beam. What does this tell her about infrared waves? ....

Q5 A **cable TV** company uses a large dish to collect TV signals from a satellite in space. It then sends these signals to houses along **optical fibres**.

a) What type(s) of EM waves could be used to send the signals along the optical fibres?

....

b) Give **two** advantages of using optical fibres to transmit signals, rather than broadcasting them.

1. ....

2. ....

Section 2.5 — Energy, Electricity and Radiation

Section 2.6 — The Earth and the Universe

The Earth's Atmosphere

Q1 Professor Gilbert is giving a lecture to some students about **climate change**. He's explaining to the students why we need the **natural greenhouse effect** and how it works.

a) Why is the natural greenhouse effect important?

....

b) Use the descriptions **A** to **E** to label the diagram showing how the greenhouse effect works. The first one has been done for you.

A The Earth absorbs radiation from the Sun.

B The greenhouse gases emit some heat radiation into space.

C Greenhouse gases absorb radiation from Earth.

D The Earth emits heat radiation.

E The greenhouse gases emit some heat towards Earth.

Q2 Some **environmental scientists** are concerned because **human activity** is **changing** the **composition** of the **atmosphere**. Circle the correct word(s) in each pair to show how the atmosphere is changing.

a) Trees naturally increase / decrease the concentration of carbon dioxide in the atmosphere. If trees are cut down more / less carbon dioxide is removed.

b) Burning fossil fuels / hydrogen releases carbon dioxide / oxygen, which increases / decreases the concentration in the atmosphere.

c) The exhausts of vehicles release carbon monoxide, nitrogen oxides and sulfur oxides. As more fuel is burnt the concentration of these pollutants in the atmosphere becomes higher / lower.

Q3 **Atmospheric scientists** monitor the composition of the **Earth's atmosphere**. They know that the Earth's atmosphere has just the right mixture of gases to maintain the conditions for **life**.

a) Tick the correct composition of Earth's atmosphere.

☐ 76% oxygen, 23% carbon dioxide, 1% nitrogen

☐ 62% oxygen, 30% nitrogen, 5% carbon dioxide

☐ 78% nitrogen, 21% oxygen, 0.04% carbon dioxide

☐ 75% carbon dioxide, 21% nitrogen, 4% oxygen

b) i) Which gas in the atmosphere, apart from carbon dioxide, is needed to support life? ....

ii) What **process** in animals and plants is this gas needed for?

....

Monitoring Atmospheric Change

Q1 Finn is an **environmental scientist**. He's studying the effect of **air pollution** in a city, on the lung disorder **asthma**. He calculates the amount of **nitrous oxide** produced by motor vehicles in the city per year and monitors the number of hospital admissions due to asthma per year.

a) Why is it important for environmental scientists to monitor air pollution, e.g. nitrous oxides?

....

b) The graph below shows some of Finn's results. Describe the trend shown in the graph.

....

....

....

c) How many people were hospitalised due to asthma in **2006**?

....

d) A new **bypass** was recently built that bypassed the area studied. Use the graph to suggest which year it was finished.

....

Q2 A **climate scientist** is monitoring **precipitation** levels in a region of a country in Africa. The graph shows the average rainfall per year for the region.

a) What was the average rainfall in **2001**?

....

b) Describe the **trend** shown in the graph.

....

c) How might this change in climate affect the people living in the region? Tick the correct answer(s).

☐ Their crops might fail.

☐ There will be an increase in soil fertility.

☐ Drinking water supplies may decrease.

☐ There will be an increased risk of flooding.

Section 2.6 — The Earth and the Universe

Monitoring Atmospheric Change

Q3 Scientists at the Mauna Loa observatory in Hawaii have been measuring **atmospheric CO_2** levels for over **60 years**. The table shows the yearly average levels of carbon dioxide in the atmosphere from 1968 to 2000.

Year	CO_2 concentration / ppm
1968	322
1972	327
1976	332
1980	338
1984	344
1988	351
1992	355
1996	362
2000	368

a) Plot a line graph of the data.

Don't forget to label the axes.

b) Using your graph, estimate the concentration of carbon dioxide in **1974**.

....

c) By how much did the carbon dioxide concentration increase between **1976** and **1996**? Circle the correct answer.

35 ppm   **30 ppm**   **28 ppm**

d) Why is it **important** to monitor the atmospheric CO_2 concentration?

....

....

....

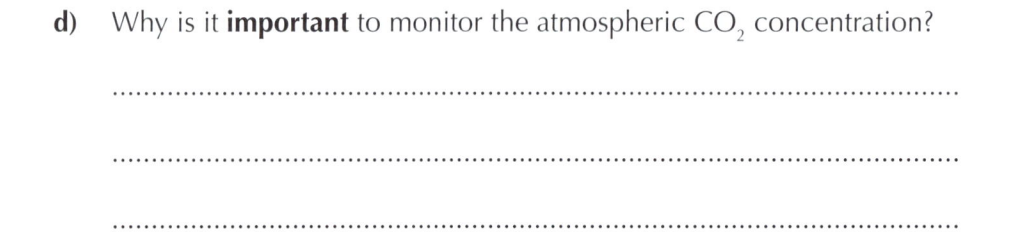

e) How do scientists find out what the concentration of carbon dioxide in the atmosphere was before modern monitoring began?

....

f) Suggest two **human activities** that increase the level of atmospheric carbon dioxide.

1. ....

2. ....

Top Tips: It's pretty likely that you'll get a data interpretation question on this stuff in the exam... But fear not — just make sure you're comfortable with reading graphs (if there's more than one axis make sure you're reading off the correct one) and describing the trends.

Section 2.6 — The Earth and the Universe

Tectonic Plates

Q1 **Geologists** study the surface of the Earth and how different features seen on Earth form.

Complete the passage using words from the box.

| tectonic | disasters | mountains | continents | slowly | quickly | plates | natural |

The surface of the Earth is composed of ....

Some changes to the Earth's surface occur .... over time and lead to

the formation of .... and .... Some changes to

the Earth's surface happen very .... and can cause

....

Q2 Fleur is a **seismologist** — she studies **earthquakes**. She's particularly interested in an area called the **Great Rift Valley**, which is the boundary between the African and Arabian plates.

Fleur **collects data** on the movement of the plates and finds out that the Red Sea is widening at a speed of **1.6 cm per year**.

a) Describe two ways Fleur could collect data on plate movements.

1. ....

2. ....

b) If the sea level and rate of plate movement remains the same, how much will the Red Sea widen in **10 000** years?

....

Remember to include a unit in your answer.

c) The Red Sea is currently exactly **325 km** wide at a certain point. If the sea level and rate of plate movement remains the same, how wide will the Red Sea be at this point in **20 000** years' time?

....

....

Don't forget to make sure your distances are in the same unit.

d) Fleur works for a **disaster management agency**. She's part of a team of scientists that monitors plate movements all over the world to try and **predict natural disasters**. Name two types of natural disaster, other than earthquakes, that are caused by tectonic plate movement.

1. ....

2. ....

Section 2.6 — The Earth and the Universe

The Universe and its Origins

Q1 The **Big Bang** theory is the accepted scientific explanation for the origin of the Universe.

Complete this passage using the words supplied below.

| expanding | matter | energy | expand | explosion |

Many scientists believe that all the .... and .... that created the Universe started in one small space. There was a huge .... and the material started to .... The Universe is still ....

Q2 **Astronomers** study all parts of the Universe.

a) Circle the correct word in each sentence to describe the different parts of the Universe.

  i) The Sun is a **star** / **galaxy**.

  ii) The Sun, eight planets and their moons make up the **Solar System** / **Milky Way**.

  iii) The Milky Way is a **Solar System** / **galaxy**.

  iv) The Universe contains **many galaxies** / **one galaxy**.

b) Complete the following sentence to describe how astronomers can study the Universe.

Astronomers use **different types** / **one type** of telescope to gather information on the moon, planets, stars and galaxies.

Q3 Simone is an **astrophysicist**. She is studying the Andromeda galaxy, which is approximately 2.5 million **light years** away.

Don't forget that a light year is a measure of distance, not time.

a) Write down the definition of a light year.

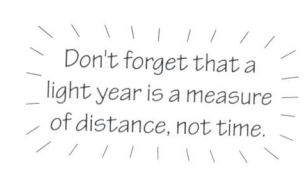

....

....

b) The table shows the distance from the Earth to different **stars** in the Universe. Put the stars in order of how far they are away from the Earth, starting with the **nearest**.

Star	Distance from earth / light years
Proxima Centauri	4.3
Algol	92.8
61 Cygni	11.4

Order: ....

Section 2.6 — The Earth and the Universe

Mixed Questions for Sections 2.5 and 2.6

Q1 Bill is concerned that he's using too much **electricity** and that it's costing him **money** as well as harming the **environment**. The diagrams on the right show his previous and current **electricity meter readings**.

previous reading: 0 0 0 4 8 3 7 . 2

current reading: 0 0 0 7 1 4 6 . 7

a) How much electricity has Bill used since he last read his meter?

Don't forget to include a unit.

....

b) Bill's electricity costs **13p per kWh**. Calculate the cost of the electricity that Bill has used.

....

c) Bill thinks he uses a lot of electricity **heating** his home. Suggest two ways that Bill could **reduce** the amount of electricity he needs to heat his house.

1. ....

2. ....

Think about what Bill could do to reduce heat loss.

d) Bill's electricity supplier generates electricity by burning coal.

   i) Which gas, released by burning coal, contributes to global warming?

   ....

   ii) What is the approximate percentage of this gas in the atmosphere? Circle the correct answer.

       0.04%   0.4%   4%   40%

Q2 Kieran runs a **karaoke** business. His equipment includes a **microphone** and some **speakers**.

a) When people sing into the microphone, energy transfers take place before the song comes out of the speakers. Circle the correct type of energy in each pair.

Speakers contain a moving part that produces sound.

microphone: sound energy → electrical / kinetic energy

speaker: light / electrical energy → kinetic / heat energy → sound energy

b) Calculate the power of Kieran's speakers if the voltage of the mains supply is **230 V** and the current flowing through the circuit is **14 A**.

....

c) Kieran could run his equipment using **batteries** rather than mains electricity. Give one advantage and one disadvantage of using batteries rather than mains electricity.

....

....

Mixed Questions for Sections 2.5 and 2.6

Q3 Jeffrey lives in **Chile**. Off the coast of Chile, the Nazca **tectonic plate** is being forced under the South American tectonic plate.

   a) Suggest two **natural disasters** that may occur in this area.

   1. ....

   2. ....

   b) Chile gets a lot of sun, so Jeffrey decides to invest in some **solar panels** to produce his electricity.

   i) What type of energy source is solar power? Underline the correct answer.

   a non-renewable energy source   a renewable energy source

   ii) Give one advantage and one disadvantage of using solar panels to produce electricity.

   ....

   ....

Q4 **Moonboots Space Centre** have sent a **shuttle** into space to do some research on the moon.

   a) Complete the following passage using the words in the box.

Universe	Milky Way	Solar System

   The .... is part of the .... galaxy. It is made up of the Sun and its orbiting asteroids, planets and moons.

   b) What is the unit used when measuring distances in space?

   ....

   c) The astronauts on the shuttle use **radio waves** to communicate with the Space Centre on Earth. Circle the correct word in the pair to complete the sentence.

   Radio waves have a low / high frequency and a short / long wavelength.

   d) The space shuttle's engine contains a **heat exchanger**. Explain what a heat exchanger does.

   ....

   ....